OBAMACARE
HEALTHCARE
APOCALYPSE

Jason Miller

A POST HILL PRESS book
ISBN (trade paperback): 978-1-61868-986-3
ISBN (eBook): 978-1-61868-987-0

Post Hill
PRESS

TABLE OF CONTENTS

INTRODUCTION

The United States Constitution—the legal document which forms the backbone of our democratic nation, the basis for which all laws are passed and regulated within the parameters of what is just and proper in a developed society, and the written memorialization of our freedoms and liberties—is roughly 4,500 words long.[1] By comparison, the Patient Protection and Affordable Care Act,[2] or "Obamacare," contains over 400,000 words! Concerned? You should be!

Much has been said about what, specifically, Obamacare requires, the changes it conveys, and the obstacles it imposes. And many of Obamacare's requirements, viewed under a microscope, are deeply concerning in their own right. But it is the cumulative effect of all requirements under this extensive federal law that may ultimately spell doom for the competitive, predominantly employment-based third-party payor[3] system in place today, thus paving the way for the government-sponsored socialized medicine that no one wants. Once you read this book, you will know the real threat that Obamacare poses to our current effective American healthcare system, why repeal is necessary, and how truly effective reform can save and supplement our current American system as opposed to sacrificing and supplanting it. And while it is preferred that you read this book in its entirety, if you choose to read only a portion, then you should read chapters 10 through 13.

Remember the old adage, "You better be careful what you wish for?" Think back along the decades before Congress passed the PPACA, the "good old days" as we will soon come to realize. Public sentiment toward healthcare waned at an accelerating pace. We saw the advent and then downfall of the health maintenance organization, better known by its acronym HMO (including early complaints by physicians about how HMOs would ruin the practice of medicine, followed later by physicians who figured out how to game the HMO model for financial gain by targeting healthy populations for recruitment); we witnessed the traditional fee-for-service methodology's effective extinction; and we saw sharp increases in our out-of-pocket contributions to premiums and other cost-sharing mechanisms, including co-payments and deductibles. At the same time, costs skyrocketed as technological advances marveled us with sci-fi-come-alive medical reality. All the while, we grudgingly dealt with a greater portion of the price tag being pushed back into our own hands because we knew, regardless of our own increasing financial obligations, that we were, and for the time being still are, the recipients of the finest healthcare in the world. The current US system may have its flaws and imperfections, but be not fooled: it is the best system in the world.

But all the same, an expectation regarding healthcare has evolved over the past several decades and, regardless of increasing costs in the realm of care, the natural inclination has been to take issue with increasing individual responsibility for a greater portion of payment. Not unexpectedly, public discord toward the status of healthcare in America marched steadily ahead through the 1980s, then quickened its pace in the '90s.

Why such increasing angst and dissatisfaction with healthcare in America? First consider that World War II–era wage increase caps thrust healthcare as an employment-based third-party benefit into the private sector by way of a "perk" for companies to lure workers from America's depleted pool of employable bodies, thus laying the foundation for healthcare coverage to become an expectation attached to employment, at least with respect to certain jobs. This expectation advanced through the prosperous 1950s, then through the '60s and '70s in a way that the obligation to pay for healthcare coverage was perceived to belong to the employer, not the individual.

But in the 1980s, care wasn't what it was back in the '40s. Medicine followed technology and had become so advanced that the price tag for coverage seemed to be reaching beyond Earth's atmosphere. Employers increased the required employee contributions to premiums and toyed with other options to contain costs or more effectively manage care, such as HMOs. Viewed as a necessity, and having been historically doled out as a benefit of employment, with wages offset accordingly, people became increasingly discontented with their coverage and their increasing out-of-pocket obligations. And so the complaints piled up, outrage became the norm, and people continued to squabble about their healthcare coverage. No one wanted to have to pay for coverage or care; people wanted to save their money for a new TV, tickets to sporting events, or a vacation rather than spend it on medical expenses or health insurance. Once again, viewed as a necessity, the expectation had become that someone else should foot the bill, and this remained the general consensus among the populous as it faced increasing out-of-pocket expenses and more elements of managed care.

By the time the 1990s rolled around, a few healthcare policy theorists and politicians began pushing hard for universal healthcare. The same populous that had been bellyaching about increasing contributions to premiums, and more hurdles and mazes to navigate with managed care initiatives, took a look at the medical situation in other countries where universal care was in place and said, "Whoa! I don't think so!" The public, as popular as it was to bash the American healthcare system, has never even remotely embraced the prospect of universal healthcare, at least not "universally," so to speak. So opposed was, and still is, the general public to universal care that Hillary Clinton's plan, viewed by many as a first step toward universal healthcare, failed miserably in Congress in 1994. Then, more recently, in response to public outrage, Congress removed the public option, which would have allowed a government-sponsored plan to compete with private insurers on an extremely uneven playing field, before passing the PPACA.[4] Where it was once chic to bash the American healthcare system, people were now fighting against the public option and now continue to fight against Obamacare.

Since enactment of the PPACA, citizens have been frantically calling for efforts to save the current system. Thus, we have come full circle when it comes to the debate on healthcare. Complaints once directed at the current American system have evolved into desperate cries to preserve it, cries that echo the fears that logically surface when faced with the potential demise of the American system, replaced in the future by socialized medicine. Remember how this introduction started? "You better be careful what you wish for."

And now Obamacare is a reality, and until at least 2016 it will reign as the law of the land in America's healthcare landscape. We must weather the storm for at least a few years, but in the fog, hail, and driving rain of Obamacare, we must not lose sight of the need to continue to push for repeal. As mentioned, much has been discussed about problematic components of Obamacare. This alone has been the basis for continued dissent by the American people when it comes to Obamacare. In fact, in July of 2013, poll results indicated that the percentage of Americans favoring repeal was at an all-time high.[5] When the truth comes out about the long-term impact that Obamacare will have on the American healthcare system, as described in this book, this percentage will grow.

There is a lot of information available about the specifics of the act, such as the income thresholds for Medicaid eligibility; the ranges for subsidy eligibility; the huge, multifaceted tax increase Obamacare imposes; and so forth. This book discusses the key components of the act but goes much further than a cut-and-dry presentation of its core elements. This book presents the theory that Obamacare will ultimately lead to the demise of the current American system. How, you may ask? This book has all of the answers and highlights the threat the PPACA poses to healthcare in America.

If this design was intentional, then the architects of the PPACA ingeniously attacked the more unpalatable aspects of the healthcare insurance industry under the veil of a constituency-pleasing consumer protection effort that in actuality is rooted in the overall objective of depleting the stability of the current employment-based third-party payor system in order to set the stage for full governmental intervention once the private healthcare industry collapses. Upon such critical failure of the current system, the government will step in with such a universal plan, fueled and financed with your tax dollars. Once again, "You better be careful what you wish for."

And note, I said the "architects" of the PPACA, not necessarily all its supporters in Congress. With such an expansive federal bill on the table, undoubtedly, even some who voted in favor of the act with altruistic intentions were duped. Be wary of a bill that spans nearly three thousand pages!

What can be said of a law that the majority of Americans oppose?[6] A law that even staunch supporters can only seem to muster a weak "something had to be done" in defense of it? Once you learn the facts about Obamacare, the truth will scare your socks off! Obamacare was designed to bankrupt the current (and effective) employment-based third-party system that dominates in America today, thus setting the stage for full-scale governmental intervention in the form of state-sponsored universal healthcare. Obamacare will shift the balance of healthcare to a government-sponsored system, funded by taxes, as opposed to reserving government programs for those who truly need them. If you work hard for your benefits as well as your paycheck; if you enjoy the finest healthcare in the world and don't want to take a number as though you were at a deli counter, only to wait for subpar care; if you care about the future of healthcare in America, congratulations! You have chosen the right book to read.

I'll say it again: the American healthcare system is not without fault, but it is the best system in the world. You may see reports that our system ranks not at number one, or in the top five, or even in the top ten, but all the way down near forty![7] Come on, I'm not buying it and neither should you! Interestingly enough, the World Health Organization (WHO), the entity responsible for this ranking, no longer utilizes the very ranking system that dropped the US model into the abyss of statistical misinformation based on questionable parameters. This abandonment followed much criticism regarding the methodology used in the rankings, so what does that tell you about how defensible this ranking was? The truth is we *do* enjoy the best healthcare in the world, as supported by public opinion,[8] and a full system overhaul that is designed to destroy the current employment-based third-party system, as Obamacare has created, was *not* the right solution. Sure, there are flaws and imperfections but we should work to improve our current system and not permit the exploitation of those minor defects to act as a springboard to socialized medicine. This book provides answers and shows how true improvement is possible without a full industry conversion to socialized medicine.

The American healthcare system can benefit from a true, foundation-up renovation, but before such a viable and effective solution can be devised and administered, one must first understand the threat that Obamacare poses today and tomorrow. Future repeal must quash the monster that looms overhead, waiting to bankrupt the insurance industry and in the interim shift the class of uninsured to the working middle class who will fund care for others through taxation of hard-earned dollars while themselves losing the very coverage they worked so hard to earn.

The Supreme Court's decision in *National Federation of Independent Business v. Sebelius*,[9] as well as the results of the 2012 election, ensure that Obamacare will reign supreme, at least for some time. Therefore, we must now weather a few years of Obamacare before repeal will be a possible option. During this time, we must remain mindful of the long-term impact Obamacare will have on our American system, as the PPACA was craftily developed with time-delayed industry pitfalls. Yes, we must continue the push toward repeal, and it is imperative that we find ways to preserve the integrity of the American system while Obamacare is the law of the land. This book will give you the information you need to keep on your toes and pull yourself out from under the cloak of deception this supposed consumer protection law has attempted to envelope America in.

You are about to learn everything you need to know about healthcare in America, the real intent of Obamacare, and how we can survive this healthcare apocalypse. This book will give you a brief lesson on the history of medicine, how and why the price tag has continued on an access-debilitating cost ascent, and how increasing discord with the cost of coverage set the stage for Obamacare. You will learn about the true intent of the PPACA and how its framers seemingly targeted consumer-noxious components of the American healthcare system. You will see that the true intent of the act, whether by design or flawed structure, is destruction of the very system it purports to reform via harsh government overregulation coupled with time-delayed implementation. You will see subpar government-based universal care looming on the horizon like a storm cloud, and you will do your part to end Obamacare. And don't worry if you don't know the difference between a co-pay, deductible, and coinsurance, as this book will give you a crash course on the healthcare insurance industry, complete with a handy reference glossary to better help you understand the business while you learn about the pending healthcare apocalypse known as Obamacare. Be informed, beware, and push for repeal!

PART I

THE PATIENT PROTECTION AND AFFORDABLE CARE ACT AND THE UNITED STATES SUPREME COURT

Obamacare is, without a doubt, historic. The PPACA constitutes an unprecedented expedition by elected officials into the American healthcare landscape. When you consider the sheer volume of content contained in the PPACA, the unending opportunities for further administrative regulation, the encroachment into personal lives by way of penalization of nonbehavior (as a penalty, not a tax, but then viewed by the Supreme Court as a tax and not a penalty), the impact the act will have on American businesses already having a tough time competing in a global market, and the practical realities concerning the legislation, you cannot help but think "historic" and "unprecedented." Obamacare is also historic in that it is an extraordinarily expansive federal step into the regulation of insurance, which has been, for the most part, left up to the states. Additional administrative burdens and regulatory compliance expenses will result since insurers will now not only have to comply with existing state laws that have not been preempted by the PPACA, but also determine precisely when the PPACA has superseded inconsistent state laws. Many insurers must also contend with further requirements established by nongovernmental entities such as the National Committee for Quality Assurance and the Blue Cross and Blue Shield Association, when applicable. That's quite the load to bear for an industry that already struggles with administrative and compliance expenses in the face of access-debilitating escalating care costs.

Equally historic is the Supreme Court decision in perhaps the most important constitutional law case of our era: *National Federation of Independent Business v. Sebelius.* Without a doubt, future Congresses will push the holding of the *NFIB* court to the limits.

CHAPTER 1

HISTORY AND CONTENT OF THE PPACA

Imagine an America where the middle class makes up the majority of the uninsured. An America where hard-working Americans pay penalties in the form of taxes that fund care for others, potentially even prisoners,[1] while they themselves cannot afford to buy coverage. Imagine being required by law to carry healthcare insurance but not being able to afford it. Imagine being penalized/taxed because you cannot afford to purchase insurance. As you look back, you recall seeking a job that provided generous benefits so that you and your family could enjoy the peace of mind that comes with healthcare coverage. However, you are now being penalized for living responsibly, paying the way for others' healthcare that you yourself cannot afford. Your employer no longer offers health insurance as a benefit, but your salary has not gone up. When you are ill and need to go see the doctor, you must wait weeks for an appointment since there aren't enough physicians to meet the demand. Meanwhile, many of those few physicians in practice have decided to operate outside of the insurance circle by creating "membership" arrangements, otherwise known as concierge practices, whereby they only see patients who pay a monthly fee. Imagine this postapocalyptic healthcare world where you, a member of middle America, are caught in the abyss of bad law. Not wealthy enough to buy coverage or purchase care, not poor enough to qualify for

Medicaid or a subsidy, you are caught in the no-man's-land that comprises the healthcare void where hard-working people reside. You are the new face of the uninsured, a member of the responsible, tax-paying middle class.

THE HISTORY OF OBAMACARE

When Congress passed the PPACA, followed by President Barack Obama signing the act into law on March 23, 2010, history was made. There is no question of this. Unfortunately, with the voluminous federal overhaul of the American healthcare system, we also met an unprecedented effort by the legislative and executive branches to seize control of an entire industry and transform it over time.

Even the passage of the act itself is mired in controversy that included party infighting and procedural strategies akin to a political chess match. The circumstances behind the act's passage—including the intraparty discussions, the vote wrangling, and the backroom deals—are enough to fill a book of its own, although one might reasonably mistake it for fiction. Once again, while clearly historic and unprecedented, Obamacare is equally detrimental and problematic for healthcare in America.

BAD INTENT OR JUST BAD LAW?

Let there be no mistake about it: there are pieces of Obamacare that are very beneficial. There are components of the act that are well-written, obviously thoroughly researched and thought out, and essentially leave almost no stone unturned on such specific points. There are important and long-overdue consumer protections written into the PPACA. On many facets, Obamacare does indeed impose appropriate regulatory checks to prevent unscrupulous practices by certain problematic insurers. But on most of these points, reputable insurers today would already have been deemed compliant long before Obamacare's inception. The free market channeling of benefit designs to marketable standards have kept the majority of the industry in check. But not all businesses have good morals, and many have and will exploit subtle revenue opportunities that can have a tremendously negative impact on an individual level in exchange for a slight per-case financial benefit multiplied across hundreds of thousands of insured lives (this adds up!) before being reined in by free market checks. So, barring overregulation, it is good to address some of these potential issues through legislation. But as the old saying goes, one bad apple can spoil the bunch, and the Obamacare basket has too many rotten apples.

The PPACA threatens the integrity of our current American system, and if left in place it will ultimately lead to a single-payor system. Considering the intricate level of detail contained in the act, it is hard to imagine that the masterminds behind it were not aware of this long-term impact. That's not to say that all those who voted in favor of the act support this end result. We certainly know there are members of Congress who want a single-payor system. Yet, considering the imposing length of the act, it seems logically probable that some well-intentioned yes votes were cast without a full realization of the long-term negative impact the PPACA will have. I don't admonish them for their efforts, those legislators who voted yes with true hope in their hearts that they were enacting a good law. But despite Congresswoman Nancy Pelosi's statement about needing to pass the bill to see what was in it, there are certain individuals, including certain think-tankers, who wrote pieces of the draft bill who knew precisely what the bill contained and likely what impact it will have on the

American healthcare system. It's simply too hard to imagine that some ideologues involved in designing the latticework of the PPACA were not aware of the risk the structure poses to the current American system. In fact, maybe the whole Pelosi statement was designed to hide the true intent of the act? Who's laughing now?

CORE CONTENT OF OBAMACARE

When you have a new federal law comprised of nearly a half million words (further compounded by references to additional federal laws, including the extensive Internal Revenue Code), from a bill that was almost three thousand pages long, what really becomes important is not simply what the law creates today but also what the law prescribes the authorities to create tomorrow, as well as the cumulative impact of all the law's nuances. The focus of this book, therefore, is not a rundown of each specific point of what Obamacare requires, permits, penalizes, mandates, warrants, incentivizes, funds, taxes, etc. This book, unlike any other on the topic, tells the real story of what Obamacare will do to the American healthcare system. Nonetheless, a review of some of the core components of the PPACA is necessary. These requirements can best be summarized under the following three categories: what Obamacare prohibits, what Obamacare requires, and what Obamacare costs.

First, figure 1.1 presents a look at what Obamacare prohibits:[2]

Figure 1.1

WHAT OBAMACARE PROHIBITS

Lifetime and Annual Limits

Section 2711 prohibits lifetime and unreasonable annual limits. This means that your insurance company cannot set a $1 million lifetime annual maximum, which would essentially leave you uninsured once you hit the lifetime max. This section also prohibits unreasonable annual limits. The lifetime maximum prohibition is much more clear than the "unreasonable annual" maximum prohibition.

Rescissions

Section 2712 prohibits insurers from rescinding coverage unless the insured has engaged in fraud or an intentional misrepresentation and also establishes certain restrictions and notification requirements for cancellation.

Medical Underwriting

Section 2701, by prescribing what the acceptable demographic parameters are when establishing premium rates, coupled with the guaranteed issue requirements of Section 2702, effectively prohibits medical underwriting. Section 2705 further prohibits medical underwriting directly. As you will learn in chapter 5, medical underwriting is one method insurers use to ameliorate risk by taking into consideration certain demographic factors relating to health when establishing a premium rate quote. This prohibition means, for instance, that your insurance company cannot take into account your diabetes when setting your rate.

Preexisting Condition Exclusions

Section 2704 prohibits preexisting condition exclusions. This means that your insurer cannot exclude coverage for your bad back simply because you were afflicted with that ailment before you obtained insurance coverage.

Excessive Waiting Periods

Section 2708 prohibits waiting periods that exceed 90 days. If, for instance, an employer requires a certain amount of time in position before coverage will commence for new hires, Section 2708 caps such periods at 90 days.

Be mindful, this list is nowhere near all-inclusive. Rather, these are the noteworthy prohibitions that are important to understanding the overall impact Obamacare will have on our current American system.

Next, figure 1.2 provides a survey of what Obamacare requires:

Figure 1.2

WHAT OBAMACARE REQUIRES

Community Rating

While the section is titled "Fair Health Insurance Premiums," Section 2701 establishes community rating with only a slight adjustment for age and tobacco usage being permissible. What this means is that insurers must charge all potential members the same rate within a set geographic region without taking into consideration factors related to health or wellness. This type of rating system causes young, healthy individuals to incur premium increases to offset premium decreases afforded to unhealthy individuals, thus arguably pricing the young and healthy out of the market and thus removing them from the risk pool.

Guaranteed Issue

Section 2702 requires insurers to accept all employer groups and individuals who apply for coverage during open and special enrollment periods.

Coverage for Essential Benefits and Establishment of a Qualified Health Plan

Section 2707 provides for coverage of essential health benefits. Section 1301 defines a "qualified health plan" under the act. Section 1302 establishes broad categories regarding such essential benefits, a condition to a qualified health plan, but grants to the Secretary of the Department of Health and Human Services (HHS) broad discretion regarding the details of these benefits.

Coverage for Preventive Health Services

Section 2713 mandates coverage for certain preventive health services without any member cost sharing. For instance, this section requires insurers to pay for a mammogram with no cost to the member. This section broadly defers to several federal agencies for determinations as to what precisely constitutes a preventive health service.

Extension of Dependent Coverage

Section 2714 requires plans that offer dependent coverage to extend to adult, unmarried children, up to age 26, dependent eligibility status.

Uniform Explanation of Benefits (EOBs) and Definitions

Section 2715 establishes mandatory uniform EOB forms and definitions.

Quality Reporting

Section 2717 provides for quality reporting requirements that place the onus on insurers to meet a broad array of quality improvement measures. This section also gives the Secretary of HHS broad discretion to establish penalties for noncompliance as well as exceptions. What is interesting about this section is that quality initiatives (which providers can more directly address) are put under the realm of insurers.

Cost Reduction and the Medical Loss Ratio (MLR)

Section 2718 addresses healthcare costs by establishing reporting requirements and a rebate program whereby insurers must pay out 80-85% (depending upon the market) in premium revenue as claims payment. This section shoulders insurers solely with the cost-reduction burden. The MLR creates an absolute cap on profits. Could the MLR actually penalize an effective and efficient insurer that has comparably low premiums and more effectively manages its cases (as opposed to paying for volume) in relation to other competitors? Is the MLR a disincentive to improving health outcomes with innovative models as opposed to continuing to pay for more and more care? This section also provides broad discretion regarding penalties to the Secretary of HHS.

Coverage for Emergency Services

Section 2719A, while titled "Patient Protections," addresses insurer obligations as opposed to provider obligations. This section provides for coverage of emergency services with the same level of member cost sharing regardless of whether the provider is participating or nonparticipating with the insurer. This section also establishes direct access to pediatric specialists and OB/GYN services.

Exchanges

Sections 1311-1313 establish healthcare exchanges on which individuals (and groups) may purchase healthcare insurance.

Medicaid Expansion

Section 2001 expands Medicaid eligibility to 133%[3] of federal poverty level. The Supreme Court decision in *NFIB* provided that states cannot be compelled to expand this Medicaid eligibility. Nonetheless, this expansion is significant. Virtually no checks are put into place to regulate this ballooning entitlement.

Individual Mandate

Section 1501 amends Chapter 48 of the Internal Revenue Code and requires individuals to maintain minimum essential coverage or face a financial penalty. The penalty, however, is very weak in comparison to the cost of coverage, it "times in" via incremental increases by year, and is subject to lighter enforcement than standard taxes.

Individual Subsidy

Section 1401 amends Chapter 1 of the Internal Revenue Code and provides for a refundable tax credit that acts as a subsidy toward the purchase of a policy on the exchange. Eligibility applies to households earning up to 400% of the federal poverty level, on an incremental scale. Section 1402 then directs the applicable health plan to reduce the subscriber's cost sharing in accordance with the eligibility requirements established in Section 1401 as follows:

- Households earning more than 100% but not more than 200% of the federal poverty line: reduction by two thirds.
- Households earning more than 200% but not more than 300% of the federal poverty line: reduction by one half.
- Households earning more than 300% but not more than 400% of the federal poverty line: reduction by one third.

Employer Mandate

Section 1513 amends Chapter 43 of the Internal Revenue Code and requires "large" employers (those with 50 or more full-time or full-time equivalent employees) to offer all full-time employees minimum essential coverage or face a financial penalty. The penalty varies dependent upon whether the employer fails entirely to offer employees a qualified health plan or whether the employer offers a plan but one or more employees obtains a premium tax credit. The cost of providing coverage will likely be greater than the penalty assessed under the employer mandate.

Small Business Tax Credit

Section 1421 amends Chapter 43 of the Internal Revenue Code to provide for a tax credit for small businesses with fewer than 25 full-time equivalent employees subject to further wage limitations.

And finally, let's look at what Obamacare costs. Now, the title of this subsection is a bit of a misnomer, admittedly. There are numerous costs associated with Obamacare, both tangible and intangible. The tax increases and new taxes imposed by Obamacare are but one subset of these tangible costs. No reasonable defense exists to counter the assertion that Obamacare represents one of the largest, perhaps ultimately the most significant, tax increase in American history. Certain taxes are pertinent with respect to the overall theme of this book and so those are the ones that are addressed here. Figure 1.3 represents a sampling of Obamacare's tax hikes.

Figure 1.3

WHAT OBAMACARE COSTS

Employer Penalty

Section 1513 amends Chapter 43 of the Internal Revenue Code and penalizes "large" employers (those with 50 or more full-time or full-time equivalent employees) for not offering all full-time employees minimum essential coverage. HHS proposed regulations provide that such coverage must not cost the employee more than 9.5% of household income and that the health plan pay for 60% of covered expenses. Here is where the penalty splits:

- If the employer does not offer coverage, the penalty is calculated on a monthly pro rata basis of $2,000 (annually) for each full-time employee. The first 30 employees are excepted out of the calculation.
- If the employer does offer coverage but does not satisfy both the 9.5% and 60% thresholds for affordability and adequacy of coverage, as noted above, and an employee decides not to take the employer-offered coverage and qualifies for a subsidy, then the rate of the employer penalty is calculated on a monthly pro rata basis of $3,000 (annually) for each full-time employee receiving a subsidy (subject to additional caps).

Individual Penalty

Section 1501 imposes a penalty on individuals for failure to maintain minimum essential coverage, as defined by the act. The Supreme Court classified this penalty as a tax. This penalty employs a "greater of" penalty utilizing a PPACA-based flat dollar amount or a percentage of taxable income (subject to certain caps). The rate of this new penalizing tax is as follows (per adult, with such amount reduced by half for each child):

- 2014: The greater of $95 or 1% of taxable income.
- 2015: The greater of $325 or 2% of taxable income.
- 2016: The greater of $695 or 2.5% of taxable income.
- Beyond 2016: Calculated with a cost-of-living adjustment applied.

The penalty is levied against the individual as well as dependents, with the penalty rate for dependents under age 18 being 50% of the individual penalty.

Tax on Cadillac Health Plans

Section 9001 amends Chapter 43 of the Internal Revenue Code to impose an excise tax on high-cost employer-sponsored coverage (or the more comprehensive plans). This is an excise tax, also known as a sin tax or vice tax. Here it attaches, somewhat atypically, to something that is neither a vice nor a sin—better healthcare coverage. Now, the interesting aspect of this tax is that Obamacare requires individuals to carry healthcare coverage, so the drafters of the bill want us to have healthcare insurance. But, apparently, they do not want us to have too much healthcare coverage; thus, the Cadillac plan tax.

Indoor Tanning Product Tax

Section 10907 amends Chapter 49 of the Internal Revenue Code and imposes an excise tax on indoor tanning services. This is also a vice or sin tax, which are commonly imposed on the overall cost of a product that is not good for us. The justification for sin taxes, which does have a sound basis, is that certain inherently unhealthy behaviors or products have a negative impact on public health, which in turn imposes additional costs on society for which we all must foot the bill. An excise tax makes more sense with respect to tanning services than Cadillac plans.

Tax on Health Plans

Section 9010 imposes significant additional taxes on health insurers.

Numerous Additional Taxes

Section 9004 imposes tax increases on health saving account (HSA) and medical saving account (MSA) distributions not used for qualified medical expenses. Section 9008 imposes additional taxes on branded pharmaceutical manufacturers and importers, and Section 9009 imposes similar increases with respect to medical device manufacturers and importers. Section 9015 imposes additional taxes on "high-income taxpayers." Section 9017 imposes an excise tax on cosmetic medical procedures.

The topic of Obamacare taxes could fill its own book!

OBAMACARE'S OMISSIONS AND RISKS

No discussion regarding Obamacare's requirements would be complete without delving into what Obamacare fails to do. In all of the words on all of the pages of this extensive federal law, Obamacare doesn't adequately address the physician shortage in order to meet the deficiency head on. Obamacare doesn't address the issue of the escalating cost of care in a sufficient manner. Essentially, Obamacare does not address the full spectrum of healthcare from patient to provider to payor in a manner that increases access, maintains or bolsters quality, and reduces or reigns in costs.

Obamacare doesn't incent all employers to provide coverage with effective tax breaks but instead forces certain employers to offer insurance under the threat of penalty (taxation), thus, tempting companies to creatively dodge the requirement by corporate maneuvering and exploiting loopholes, or to conduct a cost-benefit analysis to decide to simply pay the tax instead of the cost of coverage. (Funny how the "penalty"/tax was designed to lurk below the price point of coverage, isn't it?) Employers have announced that they will cut employee hours to avoid having to provide coverage,[4] which means Obamacare has directly reduced employment for some already. What's even more frightening is that an Internal Revenue Service (IRS) Q&A document recently released states that individuals working outside of the United States are not counted for purposes of the employer mandate.[5] How many companies will outsource the majority of their manufacturing jobs, keeping fewer than fifty core business personnel in the US, in order to avoid having to pay for coverage for thousands of employees? And how well will American companies that choose not to outsource but instead provide employees with healthcare coverage be able to compete with those that do? And Obamacare doesn't reasonably regulate draconian insurance practices; rather, it imposes its own draconian requirements on the healthcare insurance industry, requirements that may not be survivable.

WHAT WILL OBAMACARE DO?

As discussed in detail in chapter 10, Obamacare stacks the deck against insurers so that people can opt in and out of the insurance system whenever they need coverage and severely handcuff's the private insurance industry's ability to remain financially stable. Inevitably, the industry may very well fail. Obamacare effectively transforms risk, a core component of healthcare insurance, to loss. This loss threatens to tax the system (no pun intended), which today provides for coverage for the majority of people (63.9 percent in 2011[6]), to the breaking point with critical failure to follow. This massive federal law was enacted, purportedly, in large part to address the problem of the uninsured in America. By the US Census Bureau's statistics for the year 2009, just prior to Obamacare being signed into law in March of 2010, the uninsured percentage in the United States was 15.4 percent.[7] The solution? A 906-page federal law that imposes extraordinary regulatory requirements on the industry that provides coverage for the majority of Americans, rife with tax implications for individuals, businesses, and insurers.

The PPACA is 906 pages long, but the bill had a much longer page count of nearly three thousand pages. The Government Printing Office makes available a full-text PDF file of the act.[8] The 906-page law is a very "busy" document. For instance, page 125, which covers a portion of the individual mandate, contains over four hundred words!

Obamacare drastically expands Medicaid to provide eligibility to everyone with an income under 133 percent[9] of the federal poverty level. This massive expansion, besides coming at an enormous price which will be met with unprecedented tax hikes, transforms Medicaid from a last-resort, needs-based program to a choice or an option. Besides stripping all incentive to strive toward personal betterment, this entitlement program fits with the age-old problem that already plagued the insurance industry—payment for more care as opposed to better health management, starting with increased individual accountability. Whether this massive expansion is sustainable without sacrificing quality and access, and without additional tax dollars, is questionable.

The decline of the American healthcare system may wage on, full throttle, until the entire healthcare insurance industry collapses. Then in will step the government with its own plan. With the private sector lying motionless with a broken back, you will have no choice but to accept whatever healthcare the government will provide (along with increases in taxes to fund it, of course).

> Was the government option, which would have enabled the federal government to compete with private insurers on the exchanges, a red herring meant to draw our attention away from other problematic provisions contained in the PPACA, purposefully designed to be shed after absorbing the bulk of public opposition to the bill?

And so back to what Obamacare will do. This can best be summarized in two categories, as presented in figure 1.4: what Obamacare will do, and how Obamacare will impact healthcare in America.

Figure 1.4

What Obamacare Will Do	How Obamacare Will Impact America
Expand Medicaid	Individuals will weigh the cost of the penalty against the price tag for coverage.
Require individuals to carry healthcare coverage	Employers will reevaluate what type of coverage to offer, if any at all.
Tax individuals without healthcare coverage	A depletion of the risk pool, an essential element in insurance.
Require employers to provide healthcare coverage	Increases in premiums.
Tax employers who do not offer coverage	A shift in uninsured to the working middle class.
Tax health plans	A massive infusion of additional tax dollars to the federal government.
Heavily regulate the insurance industry	A striking blow to the solidity of the collective private sector healthcare insurance industry.

Following the flow of what Obamacare will do and what the impact of Obamacare will be, it is easy to see how the PPACA sets the stage for later government intervention. This is concerning, since it is a step toward a single-payor system.

CHAPTER 2

NATIONAL FEDERATION OF INDEPENDENT BUSINESS V. SEBELIUS AND OTHER LEGAL CHALLENGES

Not long after Obamacare was signed into law, the lawsuits started. Given that the PPACA is comprised of nearly a half million words of arduous federal legislation, compounded by cross-references to additional extensive federal acts, and supplemented by untold pages of regulations (many still yet to come), and considering that the majority of Americans do not favor the act, it is safe to assume that the lawsuits will keep coming.

NATIONAL FEDERATION OF INDEPENDENT BUSINESS V. SEBELIUS

At the top of the list of all lawsuits challenging Obamacare sits *National Federation of Independent Business v. Sebelius*.[1] *NFIB* was the definitive case challenging the constitutionality of the individual mandate. In what likely will go down in history as the most important constitutional law case of our era, the highest court in the land, the United States Supreme Court, examined the following significant legal issues raised in response to Obamacare:

- Whether the Anti-Injunction Act (AIA) prevented review of the constitutionality of the PPACA because no tax had yet been levied under the PPACA;
- Whether the PPACA's individual mandate is constitutional; and
- Whether Congress, through the PPACA, can compel the several states to expand their Medicaid programs by threatening to cut off states' current levels of Medicaid funding. (In order words, the states would lose the Medicaid funding they get today if they don't expand their Medicaid programs tomorrow.)

Predictions about where the high court would land on the issue of the constitutionality of Obamacare, particularly the individual mandate, varied. Some scholars speculated that the court would find the individual mandate to be an unconstitutional extension of Congress' authority and that the component was such a key and integral part of the PPACA that the entire act must be stricken. Others speculated that the court would uphold the PPACA in its entirety. Many others hypothesized that the court would "split the baby," so to speak, much as King Solomon would have done. In this case, the split would have meant that the individual mandate would have been found unconstitutional, while the remainder of the act would have been able to carry on, as the removal of the mandate would not have been deemed a fatal flaw to the remainder of the PPACA. Some even predicted that the court would delay the issue by finding that the individual mandate constituted a tax for purposes of the AIA and thus the issue was not "ripe" for review since no tax had yet been levied under the PPACA (a prerequisite of the AIA).

The Supreme Court heard just over six hours of oral arguments carried out over the course of three days in late March of 2012. America then waited and speculated about just how the court would rule on Obamacare. The wait would last nearly three months.

On the morning of June 28, 2012, the Supreme Court publicly announced one of the most surprising court decisions of all time, all contained in a packet comprised of a 59-page opinion, a 61-page partial concurrence (agreement with the majority) and partial dissent (disagreement with the majority), and a 65-page dissent supplemented by an additional two-page dissent separately written by Justice Clarence Thomas. Printed on double-sided paper, the whole thing is about as thick as a small phone book and will undoubtedly be analyzed by legal scholars for generations to come. The precedent this case established will undoubtedly serve as the rationale and justification for future Congresses to impose additional requirements via taxation on the American populous.

What makes the *NFIB* decision so shocking is not necessarily the substantive position taken by the court. The concept of the individual mandate being upheld was not an unfathomable outcome. It may not have been the most popular prediction as scholars speculated on how the court would rule, but it was not a concept left unimagined. What makes the court's decision in *NFIB* so striking is the breakdown of votes. As indicated, predictions about the actual decision the court would render varied across the entire spectrum of potential outcomes, but virtually no one predicted that Chief Justice John Roberts would join the ranks of justices taking the position that the individual mandate is a constitutional exercise of Congress' authority. One element that had remained constant between those at one end of the spectrum who said that the entire PPACA would be deemed unconstitutional and those at the other end who predicted that the entire act would be upheld was the vote count regarding the individual mandate: Chief Justice Roberts and Justices Antonin Scalia, Clarence Thomas, and Samuel Alito would vote that the individual mandate was unconstitutional; Justices Ruth Bader Ginsberg, Sonia Sotomayor, Stephen Breyer, and Elena Kagan would find the individual mandate to be constitutional; and Justice Anthony Kennedy would cast the deciding vote. The likelihood of Justice Kennedy voting no on the mandate was hotly debated before the court's decision was released to the public, but no one expected Chief Justice Roberts to cast the swing vote.

Regarding the three main legal issues the Supreme Court was called upon to decide, first was the question of whether the constitutionality of the individual mandate and PPACA as a whole was "ripe" for review under the AIA. The AIA states that "no suit for the purpose of restraining the assessment or collection of any tax shall be maintained in any court by any person."[2] What this means is that courts cannot hear complaints regarding alleged improper taxation until after the tax has been levied. Essentially, under the AIA, an individual cannot preemptively seek a court decision determining a tax to be unconstitutional before the tax is in play. The Supreme Court ruled that since the PPACA did not use the term "tax" but instead used the term "penalty," and since the PPACA does not require that the penalty be treated as a tax for purposes of the AIA, the amount that must be paid by individuals who fail to maintain minimum essential healthcare coverage is not a tax for AIA purposes.

Next, the court examined the constitutionality of the PPACA's individual mandate. The individual mandate requires most people to maintain minimum essential healthcare coverage. Failure to maintain such coverage subjects the individual to a "penalty," as the PPACA calls it and, which the Supreme Court held for purposes of the AIA, is not a tax. The government offered two arguments in support of the constitutionality of the PAPCA.

First, the government argued that Congress has authority to impose the individual mandate under the Commerce Clause[3] and Necessary and Proper Clause[4] of the US Constitution. At the risk of oversimplifying, the Commerce Clause grants Congress the authority to regulate activity that affects interstate commerce. The government argued that the failure of individuals to purchase insurance affects interstate commerce. The court noted that "Congress has never attempted to rely on that power to compel individuals not engaged in commerce to purchase an unwanted product."[5] The court then discussed prior cases upholding congressional authority under the Commerce Clause as all regulating some "activity," something that the individual mandate does not do since the failure to purchase insurance is not considered activity. According to the court, the PPACA compels individuals to become active in commerce, then punishes their failure to do so. "Construing the Commerce Clause to permit Congress to regulate individuals precisely *because* they are doing nothing would open a new and potentially vast domain to congressional authority."[6] Thus, the court held that the individual mandate is not supported by the Commerce Clause.

The government also argued that the individual mandate was proper under the Necessary and Proper Clause because it is an integral component of the economic regulation of health insurance, specifically the guaranteed issue and community rating requirements of the PPACA. In other words, the individual mandate is necessary, the government claimed, in order to offset the risk of individuals neglecting to purchase coverage as a by-product of the guaranteed issue and community rating requirements. Once again, at the risk of oversimplifying, the Necessary and Proper Clause grants Congress the authority to enact laws that are "necessary and proper" to carry out the powers enumerated in the Constitution. The court noted that its prior cases have upheld laws that "involved exercises of authority derivative of, and in service to, a granted power." The individual mandate, the court noted, "vests Congress with the extraordinary ability to create the necessary predicate to the exercise of an enumerated power." Determining that such overreaching by Congress is not supported by the Necessary and Proper Clause, the court reasoned that even if this extension were "necessary," it could not be deemed "proper."[7]

But the court determined that for purposes of determining the constitutionality of the individual mandate, the "penalty" imposed by the PPACA is in actuality a "tax" and thus a permissible extension of congressional authority under the Taxing Clause.[8] The court analyzed the Direct Tax Clause[9] and the government's argument that the individual mandate, rather than directing the purchase of insurance, instead imposes a tax upon those who fail to maintain coverage. Such a theory, the court reasoned, would mean that the PPACA does not command the purchase of insurance but rather would tax the failure to maintain such coverage. Despite the plain language of the act that individuals "shall" maintain such coverage, the court looked to whether the alternative reading of the act is a "fairly possible" one. The court looked to the structure and effect of the individual mandate and noted that while the label of "penalty" attached within the text of the mandate was fatal to the AIA inquiry, such was not determinative with respect to Congress' taxing power. In essence, the majority ruled that it is up to Congress to determine whether the AIA applies, as dictated by the label Congress attaches to a law, but that such choice of terminology does not control when determining whether a law is an appropriate exercise of Congress' taxing authority. The court then compared the concepts of taxation and penalty and determined that, regardless of the moniker attached to the individual mandate, it constitutes taxation. The court then determined that a tax imposed upon individuals for not maintaining healthcare coverage is not, under Supreme Court precedents, a capitation or direct tax and therefore there is no requirement that the tax be apportioned according to each state's population. The tax attached to the individual mandate is, the court held, not in violation of the Direct Tax Clause.

Still following it all? Under the AIA, since the PPACA did not call it a "tax," it is not a tax. Under the Direct Tax Clause, however, since the penalty functions like a "tax," it therefore is a tax.

Finally, the court examined the issue of whether the PPACA's Medicaid expansion exceeds Congress' authority under the Spending Clause.[10] Medicaid is a state program that is funded with federal dollars. The PPACA, as written, requires states to expand their Medicaid programs significantly to cover individuals who earn up to 133 percent[11] of the federal poverty level. The PPACA, as written, provides for additional federal funding for such Medicaid expansion but threatens to strip states of all their existing Medicaid funding for failure to expand their respective Medicaid programs. The court noted that today Medicaid only requires states to cover pregnant women, children, needy families, the blind, the elderly, and the disabled. Most states do not, the court noted, provide coverage for childless adults. Without accepting such expansion, the PPACA would, as written, strip states of their current levels of federal Medicaid funding. Moreover, states would be required to offer all new Medicaid-eligible individuals, subjected to the expanded eligibility, an essential health benefits package. The court noted that this expansion would result in a $100 billion increase in annual Medicaid spending. The court then noted that the Spending Clause of the Constitution and related case law permits Congress to grant funds to the states and then condition the disbursement of these funds on actions that Congress could not otherwise require the states to take. The court further likened Spending Clause requirements to a contract, and so the Spending Clause analysis hinges upon whether the states "voluntarily and knowingly accept the terms of the 'contract.'" The court then held that the Medicaid expansion contained in the PPACA is unconstitutional since it strips away states' current Medicaid funding for declining to extend their Medicaid programs. The court stated that "[w]hen . . . [the] conditions take the form of threats to terminate other significant independent grants, the conditions are properly viewed as a means of pressuring States to accept policy changes." The court classified the PPACA's requirement as "a gun to the head" of the states. In short, the court ruled that Congress cannot force the states to expand their Medicaid programs under the threat of yanking their existing Medicaid funding.[12]

Finally, the high court found that despite the unconstitutionality of conditioning the receipt of continued Medicaid funding on states agreeing to the expansion, the flaw was not fatal to the PPACA. Precluding the federal government from imposing this sanction, the court determined, is an appropriate and sufficient remedy.

At the beginning of this chapter I presented the gist of the three main legal issues the high court tackled. In a nutshell, here is how the *NFIB* court ruled on those issues:

- The mandate is not a tax for AIA purposes;
- The mandate is a tax and therefore permissible, however, under the Direct Tax Clause;
- It is impermissible to force the states to expand their Medicaid programs under threat of lost funding pursuant to the Spending Clause; and
- Despite the act being deemed unconstitutional on the Medicaid expansion issue, preventing the federal government from yanking states' current Medicaid funding as a punishment is a sufficient remedy and the remainder of the act may stand.

It is important to note that Justices Scalia, Kennedy, Thomas, and Alito noted in their joint dissent that the individual mandate and forced Medicaid expansion are both unconstitutional and being "central to [the Act's] design and operation . . . all the Act's other provisions would not have been enacted without them." Regarding the court's holding that the individual mandate was a permissible taxation by Congress under the Direct Tax Clause, the dissenters wrote: "The issue is not whether Congress had the *power* to frame the minimum coverage provision as a tax, but whether it *did* so." Applying the "fairly possible" standard, the dissenting justices determined that "there is simply no way . . . to escape what Congress enacted: a mandate that individuals maintain minimum essential coverage, enforced by a penalty." In so discussing, the dissent notes that the court has in the past found certain taxes to be so onerous as to classify them as a penalty but that the court has "never held—*never*—that a penalty imposed for violation of the law was so trivial as to be in effect a tax."[13]

> The PPACA removes the IRS enforcement tools of criminal prosecutions and levies for the individual penalty. Being stripped of the "teeth" that normally attach to government enforcement for failure to pay taxes, the individual mandate is really of limited enforceability. This all relates back to the dissenting opinion in *NFIB* regarding whether the penalty really is a tax and whether it should have been upheld.

AFTERTHOUGHTS ON THE NFIB DECISION

First, a significant component of the court's decision is that it lends support for Congress to pass additional taxes without directly being subjected to the stigma that rightfully attaches to the act of imposing additional taxes.

Crafty wording can be used to impose taxes on the people without having to vote in favor of the dreaded "T" word.

Secondly, as conveyed in chapter 10, this book poses the theory that the PPACA may have been designed to pave the way for a single-payor government-based healthcare system. The individual mandate was included to offset at least some of the inherent jeopardy that Obamacare imposes upon the risk pool, which will lead to inflated premiums and set the healthcare insurance industry into a death spin. So the question becomes, is it unreasonable to question whether the framers of the act truly expected the individual mandate to pass constitutional muster?

Finally, under the precedent established by the *NFIB* court, just how far can Congress go with this taxing structure? Could the federal government, for example, implement a tax increase (named as a penalty) and then provide an equal tax credit for every individual who agrees to be implanted with a microchip containing the individual's electronic health record?

ADDITIONAL LEGAL CHALLENGES TO OBAMACARE

The *NFIB* case was supposed to be the be-all and end-all Obamacare court challenge. The question of whether Congress has the authority to mandate some action and subsequently penalize the failure to act was a case of first impression for the high court. *NFIB* could have spelled doom for Obamacare, but it didn't. But with 906 pages of federal law and untold pages of regulations yet to come, more challenges to Obamacare will certainly surface.

The Catholic Church has been at the forefront of raising a core freedom—religious freedom—with respect to

Obamacare's requirements. As the church has noted, the First Amendment to the United States Constitution, specifically the Free Exercise Clause, prevents the government from prohibiting the free exercise of religion. Obamacare empowers the Secretary of HHS to enact nearly unlimited mandated benefits that are required in order to qualify as an essential health benefits package. This leads to employers being required to offer coverage for certain services that they find objectionable based upon their religious beliefs. Cardinal Timothy Dolan rightly classified this intrusion into our core religious freedoms not as a slippery slope but a "ski slope."[14] It's one thing when Congress, with the use of taxes, compels us to take some action that we do not wish to take. It's quite another when that very action violates our religious beliefs. Today, the required benefits might not be objectionable to you personally; tomorrow they may. As Cardinal Dolan noted, a ski slope.

PART II

THE EVOLUTION OF MODERN HEALTHCARE AND THE THIRD-PARTY PAYOR SYSTEM

In order to understand how Obamacare really works and why it is such a threat to the current structure of healthcare in America, one must first understand the basics of how medicine evolved, how and why costs are such a major factor in the healthcare arena, the basis for the dominant employment-based third-party healthcare insurance system that has prevailed for eight decades, and why we must strive to improve our current system rather than supplant it with an overhaul that threatens to tax the current system to the point of destruction with the long-term goal of full state-run socialized medicine. And this is precisely why this book explains not only the evolution of the field of medicine, with particular emphasis on significant price points on the cost escalator, but also the origins of the healthcare insurance industry, as well as a survey of how healthcare insurance functions. An understanding of these elements is imperative in order to see the threat that Obamacare poses to the future of healthcare in America.

CHAPTER 3

THE ORIGINS OF MODERN HEALTHCARE
AND THE EVOLUTION OF CARE

There was a time when medicine was more about the mystical than the scientific. Medical discoveries were few and far between, correlations between certain events and outcomes had not yet been noted, and effect was not yet synchronized with cause. Everything from organic brain disease to severe mental illness was treated by boring a hole into the skull of the afflicted individual with the intent to release the evil spirits believed to reside within. This practice was known as trepanning. In the early days of trepanning, this procedure was performed with sharpened stones. While the pain and discomfort of having one's skull slowly sliced and ground into with a sharpened flake of flint is almost unfathomable, one thing about this procedure is quite easy to comprehend: it probably didn't cost much.

Let's think about this. No expensive diagnostic testing, no CT scan, MRI, or even an X-ray; the only tool involved was a sharpened stone. The whole procedure probably didn't take more than a few minutes (faster is better without anesthesia); there were no costly drugs to administer; and there was no lengthy hospital stay, as the patient simply went home to recover or died from a massive infection or hemorrhaging. The practitioner wasn't paying off an extraordinary amount of student loan debt, didn't have to carry an exorbitant amount of malpractice insurance, and didn't have to incur the expense of maintaining multiple practice locations to serve several communities. What trepanning lacked in terms of medical efficacy, it certainly made up for in terms of cost. That's cost, in the true sense, not cost effectiveness or value.

As medicine advanced, we moved on to less severe but equally squeamish practices, such as bloodletting, whereby the practitioner would make small incisions in order to "let" a certain amount of the patient's blood out. Oftentimes, these services were performed by barbers, and at the time this probably made a lot of sense. After all, barbers already had all of the tools necessary. You get a shave, a haircut, and bloodletting treatment all at once. Once again, not a lot of overhead here. Barber tools, while more pricey than the flint cutting knives used by trepanners, didn't cost anywhere near the amount of an echocardiogram machine. The relative cost of medical care in the days of the barber-surgeon was probably comparable to the cost of a haircut today, maybe a little extra for the special treatment. (Actually, considering what we spend on hair care in this, our modern era of vanity, probably less.)

Medicine continued to progress, but much more slowly than the pace of the last hundred years. Physicians assumed the responsibility for patient care, but the practices (and associated economics) advanced slowly, at least in comparison to today's standards. And then things changed. Penicillin was discovered; electricity was channeled and used in everyday applications, including medicine; and the X-ray made it possible to look inside the human body without an invasive procedure, among other advances in science that made an impact on the field of medicine. In essence, the slow droning advance of medicine received a shot of adrenaline that came in the form of technology. Figure 3.1 marks some key healthcare advances that all occurred within the past hundred years that greatly improved public health.

Figure 3.1

Development of Antibiotics	Began with Dr. Alexander Fleming's discovery in 1928 of mold spores capable of destroying bacteria.	■ The successful treatment of bacterial infections has saved countless lives. ■ The ability to combat bacterial infections opened the door for more surgical procedures.
Imaging Technology	Just before the turn of the last century, German physicist Wilhelm Conrad Röntgen discovered X-rays.	■ The X-ray gave doctors a noninvasive way to look inside the human body. ■ Technology has since bred the development of amazing imaging techniques, such as CAT, MRI, and PET. ■ Better imaging allows for more precise surgical and nonsurgical treatment options.
Modernization of Anesthesia Techniques	Early surgeries were performed without anesthesia!	■ Advances in anesthesiology allow for surgical procedures that were not possible in the past.

Figure 3.1 represents just a small sampling of a bank of amazing advances in science and medicine that occurred just before or during the twentieth century. All of these breakthroughs utilized new and evolving forms of technology that had not been present in the past; they all facilitated an improvement in the quality of life and longevity; and, amazingly, if you plot each of these medical advances next to the corresponding costs for healthcare in America, it is easy to see that with discovery and progress comes a price. Medical advances allow people to live longer lives and become consumers of more healthcare; so, advances contribute to costs on two levels: the cost associated with the technology itself, and the secondary cost that comes with the increased consumption of healthcare services.

Technology is expensive and, in the medical setting, not self-limiting. For instance, when a new consumer product is released—let's imagine a new television that projects holographic images directly into your living room as opposed to a two-dimensional view on a screen—the new technology comes at a premium. Buy the first incarnation of this new holographic device and you will pay a fortune for it. If you don't have the money, you keep watching your now irrelevant plasma, LCD, or whatever other type of flat-screen television that was all the rage a few years ago but is now standard fare and becoming obsolete. Or you forego other more important matters in the realm of personal finance and rush out to get a television you probably can't afford.

The key issue here is choice. If you can't afford it, or if you have a well-developed ability to delay gratification and you know that prices will come down if you just wait, then you don't buy the ultra-high-tech TV set. I hate to use an old cliché here, but "you can live without it." So, the product hits the market and those who are able and willing to pay the high market introductory price do so, and as the number of individuals willing to do so slips and the company that introduced the product starts to turn a profit, the price begins to come down and the cycle continues until Walmart ends up offering the holographic projection display unit, or whatever it is called, for $249.

The scenario isn't quite the same when it comes to medical technology. The truth is, whether you can afford it or not, you don't really have the choice that you have when it comes to a high-tech entertainment item. Granted, there are overly expensive diagnostics utilized every day for pure profit motive. But there are also high-tech procedures that the recipient sometimes simply cannot live without. And so what we have is a situation where a new procedure employing state-of-the-art technology hits the medical market, and those who have a disease or disorder, previously untreatable, can now be cured or have their health greatly improved.

What they do not have is choice. It is not a matter of means to pay and certainly not a matter of choice as to whether or not to make the investment. The need sets the price, and both bad debt from those without coverage and the true necessity at stake ultimately work to keep the price for the procedure artificially high, at least in terms of value.

And so technology is the great cost inflator of advance in the medical community. Technology has converted the incurable to curable. It is at the root of development, where, for example, a single pill, which in appearance may look almost identical to the simple aspirin, may have been developed with the aid of technological advances that would make George Jetson look like Fred Flintstone. Or technology may be employed in a more direct manner, as is the case with imaging. And so, while medicine advanced much more slowly both in terms of quality and cost until about a century and a half ago, once technology entered the mix, both skyrocketed. Technology plus necessity equals rising costs.

Healthcare costs have been both incrementally and consistently on the increase since the dawn of modern healthcare. And while the progression has remained at least at a constant uphill march, at times smooth and slight, certain landmarks stick out as outliers to the gradual increase and indicate sharp spikes in the cost of care. These landmarks often show the correlation between medical advances and the associated price tag.

> Medical advances have a great impact on the cost of healthcare, but these are undeniably marvelous discoveries and achievements that tout humanity's good-natured desire to ease suffering in his fellow man. The argument should not be made that we should not strive for future advances for fear of their impact on cost. What we should focus on is fraud, waste, abuse, and inappropriate or overutilization.

CHAPTER 4

WHY IS HEALTHCARE SO COSTLY?

Healthcare is truly a unique expenditure in the US economy. It really cannot be compared to any other goods or services. Healthcare is not a commodity. It is not a luxury item. Not comparable in the least to any other service, healthcare stands alone as an island in the green sea of spending. One cannot remotely compare healthcare to other necessities, for even water, the most crucial of all basic needs, you can live without for a few days. Healthcare is not always so patient, so flexible to our needs, wants, and desires. Healthcare may be needed over the long term, or it may be needed immediately. You may not have more than a few moments to receive it, let alone a few days. Mere seconds may count. You might not be able to wait until you get that big raise to seek care. You cannot forego treatment simply because you feel the price is too high. And good luck trying to negotiate the price! Healthcare is a stubborn old mule, and it is the very nature of this true necessity that creates the real public quandary of balancing cost, quality, and access. There is no greater demand than for that which cannot be put off to another day. Only the best will be tolerated when our very lives are on the line. And, being something we "need" as opposed to something we simply "choose," "want," or even "prefer," many feel the financial burden should be a shared burden to bear. Yes, healthcare is one unique big-ticket item.

> While costly, healthcare is, without a doubt, a noble endeavor. With all the frivolous expenses in the world, when we, as a collective society, enable once incurable child cancers to be cured, is it even proper to question cost without some level of qualification?

WHEN IT COMES TO HEALTHCARE COSTS, WHAT SHOULD WE REALLY BE ASKING?

Football tickets too pricey? Don't go to the game. Colonoscopy too expensive? Bite the bullet (pun only partially intended) and go to your appointment. Just complain later about what a pain in the ass it was, both literally and figuratively. The difference here is choice. We don't choose to get sick, and we don't have much of a choice when it comes to whether or not to receive treatment. We may have treatment options, but we can rarely say no without facing dire ramifications. It is this lack of choice that complicates the typical economic concept of supply and demand setting the price. When it comes to consumer goods, choice is a critical component of demand; in healthcare, choice is severely watered down, if present at all. The lack of choice is what makes healthcare ripe for complaints about cost.

> Incidentally, "choice" as a factor in the economic concept of supply and demand does make an appearance in healthcare through the private market third-party payor system predominantly in use today. Health insurers compete with each other based upon market needs. Obviously, there is no choice in a single-payer system.

When it comes to healthcare in America, the question that is always presented is, "Why is healthcare so expensive?" But perhaps the question that really should be asked is, "Why shouldn't healthcare be expensive?" Really, when you think about it, is there any nobler of an expense or necessary a cost than healthcare? We're not discussing frivolous matters of little or no consequence here; we are talking, quite literally, about matters of life and death. We are constantly bombarded with the message of how expensive healthcare is, but consider the costs of less urgent matters. A decade ago, a federal Bureau of Labor and Statistics article reported that in the year 2000, Americans spent $203 billion on entertainment![1] And it has been shown that many people spend more on entertainment than they do on healthcare.[2] It all boils down to choice. We can say yes or no when it comes to entertainment, but not so when it comes to healthcare.

It all hinges on perspective and practicality. Regarding perspective, we perceive, and rightly so, healthcare to be a necessity. And healthcare is the truest of necessities. And we have enjoyed roughly eighty years of payment for this necessity through our employment. And I use the collective "we" since, as evidenced by a 2010 US Census Bureau report, the majority of Americans obtained coverage through employment.[3] As costs escalated, we started to feel more of the pinch in the form of increased employee contributions to premiums and other efforts geared at placing the burden for an increased portion of the costs back on the healthcare consumer, as well as efforts to incent us healthcare consumers to make better healthcare choices and thus reduce overall costs by more efficiently managing our own healthcare. General human nature creates the formula for resistance and dissent whenever such measures occur! We perceive healthcare as a necessity, and since we had become accustomed to paying very little out of pocket for our own care, either directly or through contributions to premiums, our perspective shifted from one of necessity to entitlement. We began to feel entitled to healthcare without any real obligation to contribute toward it. No one can argue that healthcare costs are not escalating at an unsustainable pace, but this perception of entitlement is what gave rise to and fueled efforts to seize control of healthcare in America. Proponents of Obamacare preyed on this perception.

Practicality enters the mix since, regardless of the perception at large, the truth is that with or without Obamacare we would not be able to stay the course. Increased individual accountability started to make its way onto the scene by way of private insurance with employers requiring greater contributions to premiums and insurers offering plans that require increased cost sharing by the insured. Increased cost sharing is one of the limited ways in which the healthcare consumer can make some choices. The consumer has a financial interest and so there is an incentive to seek economical care, such as waiting to see if your cold clears up before going to the doctor, or using a retail clinic or urgent care center instead of the emergency room for an earache. We scoffed at this and we complained even louder, and this is what opened the door for Obamacare. Now that we are beginning to understand the impact Obamacare will have, we yearn to keep that which we once complained about since we see it is a much better option. If Obamacare stands and ultimately we migrate to a full government-sponsored socialized medicine program, then where will our perception fall?

Healthcare *is* expensive! It *should* be! The argument should not be that it should not cost a lot to cure the sick, to ease the pain of those who suffer, to give a second chance to those who are staring at death's door. Nor should the argument be that people live too long, consume too much healthcare, or are too much of a financial burden on the system to be worth a few extra years. The constant bombardment on the system based upon costs, however, is not without merit. Fraud, waste, abuse, and inappropriate or overutilization are true problems and should be corrected. Obamacare does not address these issues but instead focuses on the very system that we have relied upon for eight decades.

If healthcare costs have increased dramatically while the majority of those with coverage received healthcare benefits through employment, what will the impact be under Obamacare? Right off the bat, Obamacare feeds into the entitlement perception by increasing Medicaid eligibility to 133 percent[4] of the federal poverty level. The practicality of it all is that *you* are going to pay for it, even though you may lose your benefits! How can costs be reined in under Obamacare if we have increased entitlement and threatened the viability of an employment-based third-party system, all through one of the largest tax increases in our nation's history? Dare we say that quality will surely suffer?

WHY HEALTHCARE IS EXPENSIVE

As advances in pharmaceuticals, technology, and general medical science have led to more effective, seemingly miraculous at times, treatment options, so too have costs increased in a parallel fashion. Healthcare costs can be attributed to three main components: research, technology, and education. Beyond these three dominant factors, fraud, waste, abuse, and inappropriate or overutilization also contribute, with administrative costs rounding out the equation.

Remember our trepanning example? Now let's revisit that example with research, technology, and education in mind. First, basic psychology tells us that if we do something and it doesn't work and we do it over and over again, each time we do whatever it is that is failing, the likelihood of doing it again decreases. There is no positive reinforcement for the behavior. On the other hand, if we undertake some task and have success, we are more likely to repeat the task because we have been rewarded with success. We don't have to succeed each time, but we must, at least intermittently, achieve success in order to continue to engage in the behavior. So it goes without saying that at some point, the concept of boring into an afflicted person's skull with a sharpened stone produced a favorable result. Somewhere along the line, trepanning worked. Perhaps it successfully removed pressure on the brain following a head injury and saved a life here and there; maybe it alleviated psychological symptoms from time to time, thus remedying the anomaly. The point is that at one time it worked, and more than once, presumably. What research went into this? Did some ancient physician write up a detailed hypothesis about the prospective effects of mass trepanning on the sick and injured, draft a killer grant proposal, secure a high-dollar research grant, assemble a test group and a control group, and conduct a statistically significant research study before having his results chipped into the preeminent stone tablet publication that was all the rage among peers? I highly doubt it! More likely, someone, somewhere along the line, theorized that boring a hole into the skull of an afflicted person would lead to a favorable outcome when medical or psychological issues were present and achieved some level of success in this practice. Not exactly the best research tactics by today's standards, but almost entirely without cost.

Moving on to technology, did our ancient doc employ sophisticated diagnostic equipment in order to determine that a hole in the head was medically necessary? Did he utilize a state-of-the-art operating facility, fully staffed with assistants and equipment? No, he probably just used a sharpened stone out in an open field and at best engaged the two burliest villagers to hold down the unfortunate patient for the duration of the procedure.

What about education? Did our practitioner of days gone by spend eight years in school and several more in a residency program, then maybe a postdoctoral fellowship, all the while accruing a massive amount of student loan debt and foregoing even a living wage while in training? Not likely; he probably just spent a little time with his predecessor or was just the fortunate owner of the sharpest stone in the village. No matter the case, our primitive doctor probably didn't have a lot in the way of time or money invested in his education.

Obviously it is a bit absurd to compare the most ancient of medical practices with today's state-of-the-art procedures in the healing arts, but this little exercise shows precisely how healthcare has and continues to evolve, which forms the core of increasing costs: research, technology, and education. Healthcare economists may present theories as to why costs have skyrocketed and what can be done to quell such expenses, but if you look carefully at most of these studies, they simply exploit one minor component, or flaw, within the overall grasp of the system, and the consequences of such a concept or flaw are, when considering the big picture, actually inconsequential. It's not to say that we should not be looking at these piecemeal items with the intention of eliminating waste, streamlining care delivery, and increasing efficiencies. We should—but provided the costs incurred to discover the anomaly do not exceed the savings to be found in correcting it. The problem is, a lot of the times, the individuals charged with discovering these little anomalies and correcting them (in theory at least) have careers built upon securing research grants and living off them, not maximizing the return on investment!

The simple answer is that healthcare is something that we, as an advanced and, for the most part, compassionate society, continually strive to improve. This march toward improvement means more and more research, technology, and education, and herein lies the core of healthcare's ever-ballooning price tag.

What does need to occur is that waste needs to be eliminated and efficiencies need to be maximized. There are unreasonable costs, and those must be quelled. Acceptance, however, of the fact that healthcare is necessary and will continue to be expensive is imperative, and each person must be prepared to contribute more in the future.

This leaves inappropriate or overutilization and administrative expenses. Insurance has had a role in both of these expenses. With respect to the former, insurers have created products structured around increased member accountability for his or her own health. This means higher co-pays for emergency room visits that do not result in an admission. The ER is expensive and is usually not the best choice for common minor ailments from a cost and effective utilization of resources standpoint. Administrative expenses have also plagued the healthcare industry, from provider to payor. Effective reform would address administrative expenses across the full spectrum, not just at the payor level.

> Obamacare's response? A massive expansion of Medicaid, thus fueling the entitlement perception and removing individual accountability for healthcare expenses, and the medical loss ratio which caps insurers' administrative expenses but reserves broad federal discretion to determine what constitutes an administrative expense. We can't forget the compliance and reporting costs associated with Obamacare.

HEALTHCARE COSTS AS A SLICE OF THE PIE

As we noted above, published reports indicate that Americans spend more on entertainment than they do on healthcare costs.[5] For many people in the years leading up to the passage of the PPACA, luxuries had become necessities and necessities had become viewed as entitlements. It was common to hear complaints about a $20 co-pay from someone who would spend thousands on season tickets to a sporting event. Look at where the salaries of professional athletes and celebrities have gone. Top sports figures garner tens of millions of dollars per year, and with endorsements their annual income may approach $100 million. Some actors, directors, and musicians have a net worth in the billions. We all funded and continue to fund these massive salaries. Every time we buy a movie pass, concert ticket, or piece of sporting goods equipment emblazoned with a pro player or team on the packaging, we fuel these massive salaries. We pay more than what the actual value of a product is because some celebrity uses the same model. We wear sports apparel that would cost a fraction of what it does if it bore no team logo. And all the while we complained about our $20 co-pay, or about our employer increasing our contribution to premium, or some other facet of healthcare while we still maintained great coverage, access to care, and the best quality of care in the world. We treated healthcare as an entitlement and our complaints were heard. Obamacare now threatens to replace the system we enjoyed for eight decades while retaining enough discretionary income to make celebrities billionaires. And now our collective thoughts have changed. That $20 co-pay doesn't seem so bad now. And now we fight against entitlement programs in healthcare. As they say, "The grass isn't always greener . . ."

CHAPTER 5

THE DEVELOPMENT OF THE HEALTHCARE INSURANCE INDUSTRY

Did you know that in an indirect way, the federal government created the employer-based system that dominates the market today? The same system that Obamacare now threatens to drive into extinction, thus setting the stage for socialized medicine? It all harkens back to World War II when, with a vast number of working-aged able-bodied men off fighting in the war, and with the economy booming on the home front due to the global conflict, America found herself in the grasp of a worker shortage. Competition for employees was stiff when, with hopes of funneling American dollars into the war effort, the federal government imposed wage controls. Employers were unable to financially incent, at least directly, the dwindling few in the workforce to come work for them, so other means of incentivizing these individuals became a necessity. Fringe benefits, including healthcare coverage, were not subject to the calculation for purposes of these wage controls because these benefits were considered noninflationary.[1] Fringe benefits do have value, however, and so it was the value of healthcare coverage that emerged as an attractive tool with which to lure in more employees. If both employer A and employer B offered $1.50 per hour (remember, this is during World War II) and were capped at that pay rate, then employer B gains an edge by offering healthcare coverage.

Then along comes employer C, who also offers $1.50 per hour and healthcare coverage but adds paid holidays. Employer D tacks on a pension. (Isn't it great when employers compete for employees and not the other way around?) With employers offering fringe benefits, including healthcare coverage, in order to lure in prospective employees, the employment-based third-party payor system was born. In essence, employers offered healthcare coverage as a benefit in lieu of additional wages. Our current predominant model is, therefore, a by-product of partially related governmental intervention.

Blue Cross plans are built upon the prototype developed at Baylor University in 1929 which involved prepayment for a set amount of hospitalization days.[2] In 1929, healthcare expenditures accounted for 3.6 of the gross national product (GNP)![3] But in the years leading up to 1929 and the advent of the first Blue Cross plan, medical costs were on the rise. Interestingly, a monumental event occurred in 1928 that would certainly play a role in future escalation of cost and development of the third-party payment plan—Dr. Alexander Fleming's discovery of the mold precursor to penicillin.

This system progressed through eight decades until Congress passed the PPACA in 2009 (signed into law in 2010). The federal government therefore thrust the third-party payor system into the private sector during the Second World War and then seized control of it in 2010 by mandating, rather than incenting, coverage. Even worse is the fact that the structure of Obamacare actually threatens the integrity of the healthcare insurance industry that it purports to improve through consumer protection laws. The long-term result of Obamacare may very well be government-sponsored universal healthcare. Is this merely a design flaw, a case of good intentions gone too far, or something more sinister? Either way, when you think how healthcare insurance came into being in the United States and look forward, you will see that when it comes to healthcare insurance, the feds giveth and the feds taketh away.

> Obamacare proponents are quick to point out what is wrong with healthcare today but gloss over what is right with our current system. How would we fare today if the government had taken control of healthcare in America back during the Second World War?

HOW HEALTHCARE INSURANCE WORKS

How does healthcare insurance work? The simple answer is: healthcare insurance is the buying and selling of risk. But what does this mean and how does it work? The answer is both simple and complex all at once. There are numerous intricacies within the realm of healthcare insurance that require a fair level of knowledge about the industry and the core business concepts within in order to truly understand what it really is that Obamacare attempts to accomplish and what the actual result of Obamacare will be for each one of us, the healthcare consumers in America.

First, the basics. The buying and selling of risk, which forms the keystone of healthcare insurance in America, is really no different than gambling. In essence, you, the insured, know that healthcare is far too expensive in this advanced technological era in which we live to be a feasible consumer expense. You understand that if you become moderately or seriously ill, treatment will be expensive. Knowing that care is too expensive to pay for yourself, you obtain insurance.

Most people who obtain coverage do so through their employer. You may have sought out a position that had great healthcare benefits specifically for the reasons stated above. You may have even foregone a higher salary elsewhere because you knew the value of healthcare coverage. You might work a job that is less enjoyable to you simply because you understand the value of healthcare coverage. Whichever the case may be, you have sacrificed and worked hard to make sure that you and your family will be covered in case of a healthcare crisis. You have decided not to gamble with you and your family's health and financial well-being and so you have instead chosen to gamble, either individually or, more likely, through employment-based healthcare coverage, with the insurance company.

You may now be asking how finding a job with good benefits or purchasing coverage on your own if you are self-employed is considered "gambling." It's very simple: knowing that the cost of care may bankrupt you, you have worked to obtain coverage. Your premium (and in the employer setting, the amount you are required to contribute to your premium) is the amount of the wager that you are placing with the insurer. How is this considered a wager, you may ask? Once again, the answer is less complex than you might imagine. You are betting that you will get sick and the insurance company is betting that you are not going to get sick during the benefit period. Well, realistically speaking, you are betting that you might get sick (and for once in your life, hoping that you lose the bet!) and the insurer is betting that you likely won't get sick. And that is insurance in a nutshell. Insurance is nothing more than a wager, a bet that you never want to win! All else, in the realm of healthcare insurance, flows from this very simple concept that you are betting that you may become ill and the insurance company is betting that you likely will not. Healthcare insurance becomes immensely more complicated as individual intricacies and strategies are explored, but the basic concept is quite simple: healthcare insurance is like gambling.

Another crucial concept to understanding how insurance works is the risk pool. If only you were betting against the insurance company, as a lone individual, the first time you won the best, so to speak, the insurer would be out of business. With your policy, the insurer has agreed, for a fee, to assume your risk. The risk is the expense incurred in the event that you require healthcare services. One major surgery and the insurer would be bankrupt if you were the only insured covered. But risk is managed by volume, and the collective participants in the wager against the insurer (all of the insured) comprise the risk pool. The risk pool is what allows insurance to work, i.e., what allows insurance to function as insurance and not purchased loss.

The advent of the third-party benefit risk pool model allowed individuals to receive services they would not have otherwise been able to afford. This influx of funding into the healing arts incented more research and advances since the return on investment was now there. In essence, the private system fueled research while at the same time allowing individuals to obtain advanced care, the cost of which would have been well beyond their budget. It's no coincidence that the breakthroughs we discussed earlier took off at breakneck speed in perfect timing with the advent of health insurance. Had individuals been left to pay for services themselves, science never would have advanced beyond the point of the limitation imposed by consumer financial responsibility and means. That is to say that medicine would not have evolved beyond the simple services that individuals could afford. So, in essence, the third-party payor system has financed, in part, perhaps in great part, the evolution of care in America.

> Obamacare upsets the balance in the healthcare insurance industry that had evolved through more than eighty years of free market competition.

KEY HEALTHCARE INSURANCE TERMS AND CONCEPTS

As indicated, healthcare insurance is both simple and complex all at once. The preceding section has explained the general concept of the industry in simple parlance. As we delve into more complex aspects of the insurance industry and the threat that Obamacare poses to the industry, knowledge of some industry terms will be essential. Therefore, a brief glossary is in order to serve as your guide to important healthcare insurance terms, phrases, and concepts. If you don't know the difference between a co-pay, coinsurance, and a deductible, don't worry, you will!

STANDARD INDUSTRY TERMS

The healthcare insurance industry is rife with complex terminology. The following narrative of definitions conveys this complexity in a user-friendly manner. Many, but not all, of these definitions are used throughout this book. Terms in bold are defined elsewhere in the glossary.

- **ASO:** This acronym stands for **administrative services only**. Large employer groups have a sufficient **risk pool**, which makes it unnecessary to pay an **insurer** to **underwrite** the **risk**. Since it is not feasible, however, to enter into contracts with **providers**, establish **claims** payment systems, and assume other **insurer** functionality, **ASO** accounts contract with **insurers** to perform all administrative services. **ASO** members appear to providers as, and for all intents and purposes are, essentially the same as standard **fully insured** members. The only difference is the source of funding for **claims** payment, which, in an **ASO**, comes directly from the employer.

- **Benefit:** This term has two distinct meanings. One meaning falls under the context of employment and the other falls strictly under insurance. In the context of your employment, your employer may have agreed to provide you with fringe **benefits** that may include healthcare coverage. The insurance **plan** your employer provides then contains an extensive list of items for which you have a **benefit**. For instance, you may have a **benefit** for an appendectomy but not for cosmetic rhinoplasty (a nose job).

- **Benefit Period:** This is the period of time for which the **member** is covered (or has **benefits**) as an **insured**. The typical **benefit period** is one year.

- **CHIP:** The **Children's Health Insurance Program** is a government-sponsored health program that provides free or subsidized healthcare for children on a sliding scale based upon family income.

- **Claim:** A **claim** is essentially the bill that a **provider** submits to the insurer for a **covered service**. The **claim** is subject to **benefits** determinations (for instance, whether the **member** has a **benefit** for the service rendered) and a **medical necessity** review.

- **CMS:** The **Centers for Medicare and Medicaid Services** is a federal agency that administers the **Medicare** program and coordinates with state agencies with regards to administering the dual federal/state **Medicaid** program.

- **Coinsurance:** This is the percentage of the total amount due for services rendered attributable to the **insured**. For instance, let's say your **plan** covers inpatient hospital stays at 100 percent after you have met your **deductible** if you go to an **in network** (or **participating**) hospital but only covers 80 percent if you go to an **out of network** (or **nonparticipating**) hospital. If you go to an **out of network** hospital, you will pay your **deductible** and then 20 percent of the remaining hospital bill. Let's assume you have a $1,000 **deductible** and the total hospital bill is $11,000. You pay your **deductible** of $1,000 and then 20 percent of the remaining $10,000 ($2,000 in **coinsurance**).

- **Community Rating (and Adjusted Community Rating):** In simple terms **community rating** means precisely what it sounds like—everyone in the community receives the same rate. There are no individual adjustments made for unhealthy behaviors or **preexisting conditions**. **Adjusted community rating** means that certain adjustments are made on a limited basis. Obamacare applies a form of **adjusted community rating**, with adjustments for age and tobacco use being the only acceptable modifiers to the **community rate**.

- **Co-pay:** This is the set, predetermined amount that you, the **insured**, pay in relation to each episode of care. If you need to see your primary care physician **(PCP)** for a sore throat and your plan has a $20 **co-pay** for **PCP** visits, then you are accountable for $20 for this visit. The **co-pay** applies even after you have met your **deductible**.

- **Cost Sharing:** This is the collective amount the **insured** is obligated to pay with respect to **covered services**. Typically, this includes the **deductible**, **co-payments**, and **coinsurance**.

- **Covered Services: Covered services** are those services rendered by a **provider** for which the **member** has a valid **benefit**. These services are typically based upon **medical necessity**; for example, cosmetic procedures are not considered **covered services**.

- **Deductible:** Just as you have with your auto insurance, this is the amount you must pay out of your pocket before your insurance will kick in. Let's say you have a $500 **deductible**. You must pay the first $500 for **covered services** before your insurance coverage will kick in. **Covered services** is important to keep in mind here. You can't pay out of pocket to have cosmetic surgery for which you have no **benefit** and then expect that expenditure to count toward your **deductible**. Once you have satisfied the **deductible**, it is inapplicable for the remainder of the **benefit period**.

- **Emergency:** The standard industry-wide definition of **emergency** applies a "prudent layperson" standard, which essentially boils down to whether a reasonable non-healthcare professional believes a situation to be an emergency. Of course, what is considered to be "prudent"?

- **EOB:** An **explanation of benefits** is the document that you receive from your **insurer** that says, "This is not a bill . . ." The **EOB** gives a breakdown of what the **insurer** has paid on your behalf and tells you what the **provider** may bill you.

- **FSA:** A **flexible spending account** is a deposit account whereby an **insured** can save money (without tax implications) to pay for certain **out-of-pocket** healthcare costs such as **co-pays**, **deductibles**, **coinsurance**, and prescribed pharmaceuticals. **FSA** dollars not used are forfeited after the **benefit period** (a key distinction from an **HSA**).

- **Fully Insured:** Unlike with an **ASO** account, with **fully insured** accounts the **risk** has been passed on to the **insurer** as the **underwriter**. The **insurer** pays for **covered services**.

- **HDHP:** A **high-deductible health plan** is a type of **plan** that employs a high **deductible** on the theory that it will incent healthy behavior by the **insured**, less waste through overutilization of healthcare services, and overall cost reduction through the use of the most appropriate healthcare **provider** (e.g., a physician or an urgent care center as opposed to the ER for a minor injury). Many **HDHPs** provide coverage for certain preventive services and well visits so as not to create disincentives to preventive measures. **HDHPs** also allow for lower-priced coverage.

- **HMO:** The **health maintenance organization** was a popular **managed care** structure in the 1980s and '90s. Many **HMOs** employed capitation or per-member per-month payments for healthcare services. The **HMO plan** would pay a set monthly fee to cover all members of the **HMO** who were patients of the physician. The monthly payment would be the same regardless of whether or not the member went to the physician or not. The **HMO** model has declined dramatically in recent years.

- **HSA:** Similar to an **FSA**, a **health savings account** is a deposit account whereby an **insured** can save money (without tax implications) to pay for certain **out-of-pocket** healthcare costs such as **co-pays, deductibles, coinsurance,** and prescribed pharmaceuticals. **HSA** dollars are not forfeited after the **benefit period**.

- **In Network (or Participating):** This simply means that a **provider** has entered into a contract with the **insurer** to render services for which the **insured** have a **benefit** and has agreed to accept certain rates for **covered services** rendered.

- **Indemnity (or Traditional) Plan:** This model is less prevalent today. **Indemnity plans** compensate the **insured** a percentage of what would be usual, customary, and reasonable (or UCR) for the service rendered.

- **Insured (or Member):** The individual covered under an insurance policy.

- **Insurer (or Plan):** The insurance company.

- **Managed Care:** This is a very broad concept that encompasses many existing models, including the **HMO, PPO,** and **POS** models. It is important to note that new **managed care** models are constantly being developed.

- **Medicaid:** **Medicaid** is a hybrid federal/state program. It is funded in part by the federal government but administered at the state level. **Medicaid** provides government healthcare coverage for certain low-income individuals.

- **Medical Necessity:** This is what it sounds like—care and services that are necessary from a medical standpoint. The actual meaning may vary by **insurer**, but most definitions defer to generally accepted medical standards. **Medical necessity** excludes convenience items.

- **Medical Underwriting:** Many **insurers** use **medical underwriting** to establish a **premium** rate for individual and group accounts. This rating system takes into consideration the medical history of the individuals to be covered.

- **Medicare: Medicare** is a federal program that provides healthcare coverage for individuals over age sixty-five and also covers individuals with certain disabilities.

- **Medicare Advantage Plan:** A **Medicare Advantage Plan** is a private insurance product whereby the **member** pays a commercial **premium** in exchange for additional benefits beyond what **Medicare** would traditionally provide. **Medicare** pays the **plan** directly each month for each **member** while the **premium** is used to fund the expanded **benefits** the **Medicare Advantage Plan** offers in comparison to **Medicare** alone.

- **Network: Insurers** build a **network** by contracting with **providers** to establish a contractually based rate of payment for **covered services**.

- **Open Enrollment:** This is the period of time (typically once per year) when individuals and members of groups can select their **plan** for the upcoming year.

- **Out of Network (or Nonparticipating):** This is a **provider** that has no contractual relationship with the **insurer** and thus has not agreed to accept certain contractual-based rates. In most cases, **nonparticipating providers** can bill their charges.

- **Out of Pocket:** This can mean the **insured's cost sharing** for **covered services** or amounts paid by the **insured** for services that are not considered **covered services** and are thus outside the scope of insurance, such as a cosmetic eyebrow procedure.

- **Out-of-Pocket Maximum:** This limitation applies to the **cost-sharing** portion of **out-of-pocket** expenses only. This is the maximum amount an **insured** can ultimately be liable for with respect to **covered services** during the **benefit period**, subject to annual and lifetime maximums. Typically, the significant effect of the **out-of-pocket maximum** is that it acts to cut off the **coinsurance**. For instance, the **deductible** has to be satisfied before the **insurer** pays any **claims**. The **deductible** is far less than the **out-of-pocket maximum** so it is, by design, never an issue. The **co-payment**, which can also be cut off by the **out-of-pocket maximum**, is usually a nominal fee in comparison to **coinsurance**. **Coinsurance** of, say, 20 percent can mean a substantial payment when major surgery is involved. If an **insured** has a $3,500 **out-of-pocket maximum** and requires such major surgery, the

insured is not liable for additional **coinsurance** once the **out-of-pocket maximum** has been met. Paying $3,500 is a lot less than having to pay 20 percent of a $100,000 hospital bill!

■ **PCP:** An acronym for **primary care physician**, or an insured's primary, go-to doctor for routine and certain episodic healthcare issues.

■ **Plan:** In addition to meaning the **insurer, plan** is also used to refer to the actual product, such as an **HDHP, PPO, POS,** or **HMO.**

■ **POS: Point of Service plans** pay at different amounts (usually by variance in the **coinsurance**) depending upon the location of service (inside or outside of the **POS network**).

■ **PPO: Preferred Provider Organization plans** establish differences in **member cost sharing** for **in network providers** and **out of network providers**, with **in network providers** being "preferred" from an **out-of-pocket** standpoint.

■ **Preexisting Condition:** This is an ailment or disorder that the **member** was afflicted with prior to obtaining coverage.

■ **Premium:** This is the amount paid each month for the **plan**. Essentially, this is the price of insurance. In the typical employment setting where the employer offers coverage, the employee pays only a portion of this.

■ **Provider:** This can be a healthcare professional, facility or other provider type. This is a very broad and expansive term and includes physicians, hospitals, nursing homes, etc.

■ **Risk:** In the insurance industry, the core concept is the transfer of **risk**. The individual **insured** has transferred to the **insurer** the **risk** as it pertains to the obligation to pay for **covered services** for a fee (the **premium**). The **risk** is the likelihood that an event will occur that will give rise to **covered services** and the financial obligation to pay for them.

■ **Risk Pool: Risk** is disbursed through volume, so with one individual the **risk** can be very high. The more individuals the less overall **risk** (subject to certain other industry safeguards). The **risk pool** is therefore all the group of **insured** who have been offered coverage subject to other industry safeguards, such as **medical underwriting** and/or **preexisting condition** exclusions.

■ **Underwrite:** To **underwrite** means the **insurer** agrees to take on the financial **risk**, or to be liable for **claims**.

PART III:

HEALTHCARE IN CONTEMPORARY TIMES: COST, QUALITY, ACCESS, AND THE EMPLOYMENT-BASED THIRD-PARTY PAYOR SYSTEM

Nearly all difficulties within the healthcare industry can be traced back to the triumvirate of the American healthcare system: cost, quality, and access. These three components often compete against each other in an autoimmune melee. It is the perfect balance between these three difficult and demanding concepts that the industry has searched for decades. A unique attribute of the American third-party payor system is that market forces intercede to impose some level of competitive balance to the mix. If the consumer market demands increased quality, then the consumer market infuses additional dollars into the mix. If the consumer market wants a more economical model, then payors respond by offering products with more cost sharing imposed on the insured. In a single payor system, one entity alone, the government, makes all decisions impacting cost, quality, and access. This model is not conducive to change to reflect market needs and desires.

CHAPTER 6

COST, QUALITY, AND ACCESS: BALANCING NECESSITIES AND JUGGLING PRIORITIES

Cost, quality, and access; it's hard to believe that these three simple words create a formula so complex, a conundrum of unparalleled dismal comparison in any industry, an enigma with far-reaching consequences into our everyday lives. But they do! These three, often competing interests and objectives form the crux of America's healthcare dilemma: that is, the difficulty faced in achieving cost effectiveness while maximizing quality and access. Think about the bare necessities in life: food, clothing, and shelter. Now think about obtaining these three necessities on a limited budget, which is a stark reality for an increasing number of Americans each year. If you have $1,000 per month to work with and rent costs $600 and food costs $300, then quite simply you only have $100 left for clothing. If your landlord raises your rent to $650 and the cost of food increases to $325, then your monthly allotment for clothing drops to $25. You have to eat and you need a roof over your head, so you balance your necessities and reduce your spending on clothing. Now you wait three or four months and then buy even more economical clothing than you had purchased in the past. Once again, you are balancing necessities. Now, obviously, this is an oversimplified example, but it illustrates the point of how difficult it can be to balance necessities without the added complexity cost, quality, and access impose in the healthcare arena.

Now, if the $25 per month does not afford you the opportunity to look presentable at work, and thus decreases your chances for advancement, then you might decide to sacrifice on the quality of your shelter by finding a cheaper apartment. If you find a smaller apartment for $500, as cramped and uncomfortable as it may be, then you free up another $150 per month for clothing. You can now buy more appropriate attire for the workplace in the hopes of ultimately being promoted, not because of your new look, but without the hindrance of your old one. You can also free up additional funds by adopting a more economical diet. What college student hasn't done precisely this with the scrumptious ramen noodle diet? You may not be eating well, but you derive sustenance. You have juggled your priorities as your situation has dictated. You have made a decision to make a sacrifice with respect to one or more necessities in order to fuel another priority, all in an effort to bolster your professionalism at work because you are thinking about long-term success, which will mean more financial resources to meet life's needs.

We have all balanced necessities and juggled priorities. It is neither a fun nor easy thing to do! But in the foregoing example, it is all pretty cut and dry: X dollars to fund Y priorities. As variables are introduced, the distribution shifts. This may require taking funding away from one necessity to pay for another, or downgrading a particular necessity in order to be able to afford all three necessities. It may not be easy, but it is all pretty clear.

HEALTHCARE: A CONFLICT IN NECESSITIES

Think about the above example. We have all been faced with a similar balancing and juggling act at some point in our lives. Now consider how much more complex the whole situation becomes when we introduce the ultimate complicating factor: in the collective healthcare realm, the necessities not only compete with each other for limited resources but they actually conflict with each other at times! Think about it: if access goes up (a good thing), then so do costs (not a good thing) and perhaps quality suffers (also not a good thing). If we cut costs (a good thing), then less access and lower quality may result (certainly not a good thing). If we improve quality (a good thing), then costs rise (not good) and access may drop as a result (also not good). This dilemma is illustrated in Figure 6.1.

Figure 6.1

Increased Quality	Often comes at an increased cost because of the research, technology, and education costs associated with increases in quality.	Which in turn may reduce access because of the higher price tag.
Increased Access	Means costs go up because more people are accessing healthcare services.	Which may mean a decrease in quality if supply is not commensurate with the increased demand level.
Decreased Costs	May increase access since healthcare is more affordable.	But with less influx of funding, may result in lower quality.

It is almost as though we have three parasites all feeding off each other trying to survive!

Now recall the "college ramen" diet mentioned above. You reduce costs associated with feeding yourself by adopting a much more economical diet. Now, as long as you don't exclusively live on ramen noodles, you can adopt a more economical diet and live well. The quality, as measured by taste, may subside but the quality, as measured by nutritional value, may remain level or even increase (costly meals are not necessarily healthier ones). Think about healthcare as a comparison. There isn't always a less costly substitute! If you require heart surgery, there aren't a lot of less costly yet equally effective options available.

Just when you thought it wouldn't get any more complicated, another concept enters the fray! Every purported benefit in the above illustration (i.e., increase in access being a good thing, cutting costs being a good thing, and improved quality being a good thing) is based upon a flawed supposition! Increased access is only a good thing when healthcare is accessed appropriately. If everyone runs to the doctor every time he or she has a cold, or a stubbed toe, or a splinter, just because there is more access, that is *not* a good thing. If we indiscriminately cut costs without managing healthcare more efficiently (even though this may appear to be a good thing in the books) in terms of value, it is not. If we improve quality in one area while other more pressing quality concerns persist and fester, we have not accomplished anything great. You wouldn't buff the bumper on a rusted out '73 Ford Pinto, would you?

Just when you thought it was complex enough, factor in the reality that each of these three components are in a constant state of flux and vary based upon subjective viewpoints. The individual will gauge quality in terms of the care he or she receives. Public health officials look at the collective health of the population. This shows the subjective nature of cost perception in healthcare. And what was considered state of the art twenty years ago might be antiquated and outdated today, showing that quality in healthcare is constantly changing. By comparison, if you supplement the ramen diet with some fresh vegetables and fish, then it is objectively a healthy diet today, tomorrow, and twenty years from now (it is objective and a constant).

TRUE IMPROVEMENTS, NOT MERELY PERCEIVED ONES

In order to even begin to tackle the monstrous task of balancing these three equally important but often competing necessities, we must first acknowledge some important facets of this dilemma. First, increased access, *on its own*, should not by default be labeled a good thing. Increased access must be tempered with some level of individual accountability, both financial and with respect to the decision-making process. If you have 100 percent coverage at no out-of-pocket cost whatsoever (no contribution to premium, no co-pays, no deductible, no coinsurance), are you going to access the healthcare system in an economical fashion? Are you going to make a doctor's appointment when you have an earache and wait until the next day when the first appointment is available, or are you just going to run to the emergency room and obtain a prescription the same day? Are you going to look for a cheaper solution, such as a retail clinic or urgent care center, or are you going to just go to the ER because it is closer? If you have a high-deductible health plan, I bet you will take a much different approach! But the bar should not be set too high either. We don't want bronchitis turning into pneumonia because the patient waited because the financial burden fell solely upon his or her shoulders.

Increased access, when it doesn't flood the system with an overabundance of unnecessary care, and when patients are encouraged to make wise healthcare choices, is a *great* thing, not simply a good thing.

Costs, costs, costs! This is a biggie when it comes to healthcare in America. But simply cutting costs isn't necessarily always a good thing. If a service, while expensive, is efficiently administered, effective, and in the long run prevents other more expensive future procedures, then no gain is to be had here. There simply is no fat to trim. The goal should be to control costs, not blindly cut them. The focus should be efficiency and value, not strictly dollars and cents.

Is there value in cleaning the window when you can see through it just fine? Sure, it may technically now be without those two minor smudges, but was it necessary? Improvements in quality in the healthcare setting are of paramount importance. But what do we gain in tweaking an already adequately effective procedure? Particularly if there are other areas of more pressing concern? Have we really improved quality if we have simply painted over the rust?

PRIORITIES IN PERSPECTIVE

It is also noteworthy to discuss the role of perspective when considering priorities in healthcare. First, which of these three qualities of healthcare is the most important? A very simple question to ask, but the answer is not so simple. For instance, if you were right now lying on the operating room table, breathing in the anesthetic, about to have your appendix removed, I don't think you would be too concerned about access and cost. For one, access would not be an issue for you at the moment. You're on the table, the anesthesiologist is doing his job, and the surgeon is on her way in to do hers. Access isn't an issue for you at present because you are already actively engaged in receiving the care that you need. Nor would you likely be thinking about cost at this point. Once that pain in your lower right quadrant kicked in and brought you to your knees in a shivering cold sweat, who was going to pay for your appendectomy slid way down the scale on your list of priorities. You just want the pain to go away, regardless of cost. Besides, at this point, you either have healthcare coverage or you don't. If you do, you are already prepared to meet your out-of-pocket liability; if not, the bill is going to be far too high to pay and you will likely need to file for bankruptcy to wipe out the debt. Either way, not your number one priority at the moment.

Now imagine you are a different person, in a different time. You are your boss, three months before your appendix went sour. You are shopping for economical healthcare coverage for your employees. You have a budget, and the quotes for coverage for the same plan you had in place last year are high. Is quality still your number one concern? Now, unless you are Ebenezer Scrooge, you are likely still concerned about quality, but I suspect that cost is currently your number one concern.

Now imagine that you have fully recovered from your appendectomy and you are doing some yard work and you hurt your back. You call your doctor and the earliest that he can see you is in three weeks. I'll bet access is your number one concern as you deal with the excruciating pain in your lower back.

Cost, quality, and access. There is no uniformity; there are no certainties; nothing remains constant. Which of these three important concepts in healthcare is the most important may change as the wind blows. They may rank differently between different individuals in different roles and performing different functions. They may change for a lone individual based upon different circumstances and needs. This dilemma, how to balance these three ever-changing, often competing interests, is what makes solving the healthcare issue in a truly effective way such a difficult task to achieve.

Increase access and quality may slip. Moreover, unless cost can be controlled with the increased access, cost will also rise. Manage cost and quality may diminish. So, too, may access, if the cost management measures put providers out of business. Tackle quality issues and cost may increase. Access may decrease, too, if it becomes too cumbersome for providers to manage quality on a greater scale.

OBAMACARE'S RESPONSE AND UNRESPONSIVENESS

To be perfectly honest, we cannot address Obamacare's response to the cost, quality, and access issue, including the problematic issues Obamacare will present, without also discussing Obamacare's lack of a response, or Obamacare's unresponsiveness, when it comes to cost, quality, and access.

We have seen attempts to strike a balance between these three interests come and go. Some have achieved a level of success; others have not. With Obamacare, several things are certain: (1) Obamacare doesn't address healthcare sufficiently across the entire spectrum; (2) increased regulatory action in the form of Obamacare will make striking this crucial balance more difficult, if not impossible; and (3) Obamacare's massive Medicaid expansion will perpetuate overutilization, which will have an adverse impact on cost, potentially flood already scarce provider resources, and cause quality to take a downturn as more dollars will be channeled into providing more care, not necessarily appropriate care.

To elaborate, Obamacare does not begin at the root of the issue; rather, Obamacare attacks the industry that is ripe for criticism: the healthcare insurance industry. The suspected true motives and the long-term effects of Obamacare's approach are set forth in part 4, but what must be stated here is that effective reform cannot threaten our imperfect but effective third-party payor system.

Moreover, extensive legislation and additional requirements, without attempting to improve care from delivery on up, will not even remotely improve the cost, quality, and access balance. More funds will be rolled into penalties (taxes) and into compliance than into improving efficiency of care delivery. This will further divide this triumvirate of healthcare in America and we will actually see the unthinkable happen: lower quality, higher cost, and less access!

How can Obamacare do this, you may ask? Here's how. Obamacare's massive Medicaid expansion converts Medicaid from a quasi-needs-based program to a flat, income-based entitlement program. If the cost, quality, and access balance has been a struggle with our current system that has evolved to engage the consumer in wise healthcare decision making and personal accountability, then what will the effects of this entitlement program be?

Only time will tell the full impact of Obamacare on cost, quality, and access, but figure 6.2 sets forth some issues to consider.

Figure 6.2

Cost
- Massive Medicaid expansion
- An individual penalty
- An employer penalty
- A host of new taxes and tax increases

Quality
- Entitlement programs = decreased individual accountability
- Increasing governmental obligations for payment may impact the federal research grant program.

Access
- Extensive federal legislation designed to regulate the industry that already provides coverage for the majority of Americans.
- A full migration to single payor may mean more theoretical access, but socialized medicine models in foreign nations illustrate issues with the ability to access services.

The crucial balance between cost, quality, and access absolutely must address efficiency of care. Maximize efficiencies in care delivery, administration, claims payment, and all other facets of the full spectrum that is healthcare in America and you will have struck the balance between these three uncooperative beasts. Helping our current system find a way to navigate these difficulties is the answer, not extensive federal regulation of the industry that today provides coverage for the majority of Americans.

CHAPTER 7

INSURERS: THE EASY TARGET, BUT . . .

Let's face it, certain individuals and entities are just easy to target as the "bad guys." Banks, credit card companies, attorneys, and, yes, health insurance companies are easy to point the finger at without much backlash. The media targets them, the general public admonishes them, and it is generally acceptable within the confines of our mostly civil society to attack them both in jest and with true animosity. These individuals and entities make up the collective easy target. In healthcare, insurance companies sit alone in this role.

Now, within the confines of the healthcare arena, we have many players involved. First, we have the patient. This is the unfortunate individual who is the victim of some illness or injury. Not only a human being, but a sick human being, in need and deserving of our compassion and comfort. Certainly, the patient is no easy target. In fact, the patient is pretty much off limits entirely when taking stock of America's healthcare woes. Regardless of whether the patient's own unhealthy lifestyle choices contributed to or even solely caused the patient's current healthcare dilemma, the patient cannot be targeted. At best we can perhaps address the individual and his or her own well-being and contribution to such well-being through healthy living choices, or the lack thereof, in the collective. We can say that we all need to get out and get more exercise and eat better, but the patient, as an individual, remains off limits, and the person who makes unhealthy choices, while fair game for some light prodding, is certainly no easy target.

Following the route of natural progression, where does the patient go when ill? Naturally, to the provider. In the old days I would have said to the doctor or hospital, but ours is an era of expanding roles for non-physician practitioners and multiplying options for care delivery settings with the advent of urgent care centers, retail clinics, and a bevy of additional options that vary by case as opposed to the traditional choices. The provider—and for this illustrative example, let's assume a physician—may be very well off financially. He may drive a very expensive car, he may wear a very expensive watch. He may be arrogant, he may be egotistical. He may even be motivated by factors completely outside the realm of the Hippocratic oath. He may be more engaged in the practice of business than of medicine and focused solely on profit. But, except for in the most extreme, heinous cases, the practitioner is never the easy target. Regardless of salary, these are individuals who have worked hard and sacrificed to join the healing arts. They work long hours and give up a lot of personal time. Their families make do with absences from the dinner table, Little League games, and recitals. Sure, a few may be misguided but most are not. Some light chiding about salaries and Wednesday golf aside, the provider is certainly no easy target.

And so as our little example goes the patient went to the provider and received treatment and is now all better. Now it's time for the bill. Who steps up to the plate? If the patient has healthcare coverage, the insurance company does, of course. The insurance company is tasked with paying the bills for eligible, covered services that are the result of the member's having received such treatment. The truth be told, insurance companies are not printing presses. Insurance companies are in business and strive to stay in business, something which cannot be accomplished if certain checks and balances are not put into place; something that will be a short-lived venture if the business practice is to blindly and unquestioningly write checks to providers. And this is where we find our resident bad guy in the field of healthcare, and here's why.

First, the insurance company is not a person, it is a company. A cold, impersonal entity organized as a corporation and in business for the sole purpose of making money. This is the common perception, mind you, not necessarily reality. Secondly, the insurance company doesn't treat or heal, at least not directly. The insurance company doesn't come into play until after services are rendered, or, if they do enter the mix beforehand, it is to deny a service before it is even rendered (once again, at least as common perception would have it). This further thrusts this dark being into the role of villain. These common perceptions work to vilify insurers beyond any blame actually due them. And finally, the insurance company has adversaries out on the front line. Oftentimes these are the same providers discussed in this chapter. These providers are people, they heal, and they are not perceived as bad guys. And they have the patient's ear. So when the insurer pays a rate for a service the provider doesn't like, whether the rate is fair or not, the provider complains to whom? You guessed it, the patient!

Some insurers deserve the blame they receive. But, unfortunately, we have let a few bad apples spoil our perception of the entire bunch. Some are motivated primarily by profit, having lost sights on the overall goal within the realm of healthcare. While the goal of maintaining and sustaining profitability is not a bad thing, excessive practices based in greed is a different story.

But not all insurers are evil corporate empires driven solely by yearnings to maximize profits; not all insurance practices are designed to stick it to the American worker. A common theme presented in this book is that insurance is the transfer of risk in exchange for money. In order to remain financially viable and thus sustain the ability to keep premiums as low as possible, certain industry safeguards have developed over the years. Certain insurers have absolutely engaged in deplorable business practices over time, but the majority of insurers have adopted relatively necessary practices that may prove frustrating to certain individuals on a case-by-case basis but have allowed for coverage to be obtained en masse in an economical fashion. What also makes insurers such an easy target is that ultimately their product is payment for medical services and, based upon certain industry safeguards, sometimes payment is denied. The insurer's role is not a pretty or easy one, but the greater good they serve is often lost on an individual, case-by-case basis.

The insurance industry as a whole has done a great job of managing risk, pooling members together, paying for services, and thus infusing money into healthcare, which is often rolled back into research and development that, in turn, increases quality. Premiums for a thousand insured pays for the costly services incurred by those of the thousand who become sick or injured, thus injecting revenue back into the care system to be used in part to fund yet further advances. This allows those in need to receive services that they would not have been able to otherwise afford on their own.

There are many insurance companies that have actively engaged their members to improve their health, and thus have changed the focus of modern insurance from simply paying for services rendered to preventing illness, maintaining health, and ensuring value for healthcare dollars spent as opposed to simply paying for more and more utilization of services. Do you remember visiting sick friends or relatives in the hospital? It wasn't all that long ago that the standard course in the medical profession was to admit patients to the hospital and keep them there while they underwent all necessary tests. Relatively "well" people would spend a week in the hospital, potentially acquiring additional hospital-based infections. It was the insurance companies that began to curb the practice of keeping patients in the hospital for as long as possible, much to the chagrin of providers, and the serendipitous result was that oftentimes the outcomes improved because the patients weren't subject to as many hospital-based infections and were more comfortable at home. Granted, the insurers were probably not completely altruistic in their motives on this one, but they recognized that, perhaps, neither were providers when it came to the old practice of keeping patients in the hospital.

So, if you must view insurers as evil, at least understand that they are a necessary evil and a core player in the best healthcare model in the world. One need look no further than the Medicare Advantage Plan program, which fills in the gaps left by a government-based healthcare program. Preservation of the financial integrity of insurers is crucial, and sometimes the means by which this is achieved are not pretty. But the difficult and often unattractive task of effectively managing risk is precisely what has permitted coverage for the majority of Americans over the last eight decades.

CHAPTER 8

CURRENT HEALTHCARE INDUSTRY STANDARDS AND PRACTICES:

A SURVEY OF THE NECESSARY
AS WELL AS THE CHAOTIC

There is no doubt that over the eight decades of evolution of the American healthcare system, certain insurance industry standards and practices have evolved that are less than attractive to the public. The framers of Obamacare knew this and pounced upon these very practices. And while certain reasonable restrictions may be of value, the flat-out prohibitions and restrictions Obamacare imposes upon the insurance industry as a whole, and as explained in detail in part 4, presents a dangerous threat to our healthcare system.

It is important that we all understand why these practices evolved the way they did, the intent behind them, how they function, and how they can actually lead to more coverage, considering the big picture, and not less. Yes, at times, while chaotic, these very standards and practices are often necessary.

It is these very practices that are ripe for criticism that the framers of Obamacare exploited in order to build a legislative framework that appears to provide consumer protections but in reality goes way too far and will ultimately break the spine of the healthcare insurance industry. That's why it is imperative to understand how and why these practices evolved, how they work, and where the line falls between effective regulatory control and crippling overregulation. To facilitate understanding of these necessary evils and how they permit coverage for more individuals rather than less, a review of two such components, which will be banned outright beginning in January of 2014, is appropriate: preexisting condition exclusions and medical underwriting.

PREEXISTING CONDITION EXCLUSIONS

The concept of preexisting condition exclusions evolved to prevent individuals from waiting until becoming sick before obtaining healthcare coverage. Think about it: if no ailment may be excluded from coverage, how does this impact your incentive to obtain coverage? If you know that if you get sick or injured you can simply buy insurance that will cover treatment for the illness or injury, why not wait until you need coverage to purchase it? If you are young and healthy, what is your incentive to maintain healthcare coverage? After all, there are a lot more fun things to spend your money on!

Remember, insurance is all about the transfer of risk. Furthermore, the backbone of the insurance industry is the management of risk, and building an effective risk pool is the cornerstone of this concept. By prohibiting coverage for ailments that precede the date of coverage, preexisting condition exclusions incentivize healthy individuals to obtain coverage and enter the risk pool. This helps permit insurance to function as insurance. This requirement obligates individuals to obtain coverage before the event (the ailment, that is) comes into being; otherwise, the insured would simply be paying a lesser amount in the form of a premium for payment for a known medical issue. For insurers, this is no longer insurance with the buying and selling of risk; rather, it devolves into purchasing payment for your healthcare bills at a fraction of your liability, sort of a parallel opposite of buying bad debt for pennies on the dollar. This is no longer insurance; this is guaranteed loss.

Have certain insurers gone too far with preexisting condition exclusions? Certainly. However, preexisting condition exclusions, at least on some level, constitute a necessary evil for the survival of a viable third-party payor system. Chapter 10 delves into this issue, and others, with a focus on the long-term cumulative impact of Obamacare's stringent requirements.

MEDICAL UNDERWRITING

Remember, medical underwriting involves looking at the insured's medical background in order to establish a premium rate that is synchronized with the risk attached to such individual. On the other end of the spectrum is community rating, which means, simply put, that everyone in the community receives the same rate without regard for the health of the individual. Adjusted community rating is community rating with a minor adjustment or two for such things as smoking.

Medical underwriting evolved in order to predict, essentially, health outcomes for individuals based upon their health status. Based upon the predictions, a corresponding rate would be established. If you took good care of yourself, the more likely you would be to receive a favorable rate than if you were overweight, smoked, and did not exercise. Medical underwriting, therefore, incentivizes healthy living.

Just as with preexisting condition exclusions, certain insurers have gone too far with medical underwriting in the past. But the outright prohibition Obamacare imposes presents the risk of skyrocketing premiums for the young and healthy, thus creating a disincentive for these individuals who otherwise balance out the risk pool from carrying healthcare insurance.

OBAMACARE'S RESPONSE

Does Obamacare address, in a reasonable manner, these practices in order to curb chaotic outcomes while preserving the integrity of the current employment-based system? No, Obamacare flat-out outlawed these practices. This dramatically decreases any incentive on the part of individuals to maintain coverage. Individuals have less risk if they choose to stay out of insurance while healthy. This cuts against the grain of the core backbone behind insurance: that healthy individuals offset the risk posed by the sick. By staying engaged in insurance, when the young and healthy age and their health deteriorates, a new crop of young and healthy individuals enter the system and offset the risk posed by the now high-risk individuals. Moreover, the impact of these prohibitions will mean fewer people in the third-party payor system; specifically, fewer "good risk" individuals. The ramifications are twofold: less revenue because of fewer insured, and more claims payments based upon a less effective risk pool.

What would be a more reasonable approach to curtail the chaotic practices of some insurers when it comes to preexisting condition exclusions? Well, first of all, most states already have imposed limits on the time period for which insurers may impose preexisting condition exclusions. But accepting for argument's sake the need for uniformity on this issue, how could healthcare reform address this issue without risking breaking the back of the industry? The options are nearly endless, and all involve some reasonable limitation or safety valve. These include:

- A universal time limitation on preexisting condition exclusions

- An exemption for certain life-threatening conditions

- A quasi-prohibition that restricts insurers from imposing such restrictions but permits insurers to impose significantly higher cost sharing, such as a higher coinsurance percentage. This would not only incent individuals to not wait until sick to obtain coverage but would allow them to receive the services they need while, fairly so, bearing more of a financial burden.

As you can see, the options are endless. It would not have been difficult to impose reasonable limitations with adequate industry-preserving safety valves in place. And remember, Obamacare's authors did include a safety valve when it comes to the Medicaid expansion. While the requirement to expand Medicaid programs in order for states to remain eligible to receive current Medicaid program funding was deemed unconstitutional by the Supreme Court, already in place was a second tool by which to expand Medicaid: the financial inducement in the form of additional federal dollars for the expansion. This shows that the PPACA was thought out very well, which brings the motive behind the act into question.

The same type of reasonable regulatory structure could have been imposed with respect to the permissible form of underwriting. Do adjustments for age and tobacco use provide enough variance to entice young and healthy individuals to join the risk pool and thus balance out the risk, thus enabling the system to remain viable and intact, thus funding care for those who need it? Doubtful. Some reasonable middle ground exists on both of these issues. Obamacare misses the mark on each.

Insurers are permitted to charge higher premiums for tobacco use subject to a "1.5 to 1" ratio. This means the premium can be 50 percent higher for tobacco users. Interestingly enough, the PPACA does not appear to provide for a similar surcharge for Medicaid-eligible individuals who use tobacco. Wouldn't an additional excise tax on tobacco products be more effective, fairly applied, and further removed from avoidance by individuals who may simply deny using tobacco products to obtain a more favorable premium?

Remember, these two components directly impact insurers' ability to manage risk. These very components are so intertwined in the core functions of insurance that they are not limited to healthcare insurance. Consider life insurance, for instance. Underwriters look at medical histories, age, and other factors before offering a life insurance policy. Once again, these practices may not be pretty, and there is room for reasonable controls to be put into place. But blanket prohibitions risk the system that today provides coverage for 63.9 percent of Americans.[1]

PART IV

THE PATIENT PROTECTION AND
AFFORDABLE CARE ACT:

THE TIME BOMB SET TO BANKRUPT THE
HEALTHCARE INDUSTRY

So far we have explored the bulk of Obamacare's key provisions; we have gone back in time to healthcare's modest beginnings and followed its miraculous evolution to present-day medicine, observing the corresponding increases in costs; we have explored the dilemma created by the need to balance cost, quality, and access; and most importantly, we have followed the evolution of the employment-based third-party payor system that dominates in America today. We have seen how the evolution of this system has permitted the majority of Americans to obtain healthcare services they would not have otherwise been able to afford. Now it is time to consider the long-term impact Obamacare will have on this system and how the PPACA poses a real threat to healthcare in America.

CHAPTER 9

PROBLEMATIC COMPONENTS OF THE PATIENT PROTECTION AND AFFORDABLE CARE ACT

Before we can even begin to discuss what is problematic with respect to Obamacare's precise requirements, we must first realize that the overall design of the PPACA in and of itself is highly problematic. The long-term impact of Obamacare, quite possibly by intentional design, will be traumatic for the current American healthcare system. What is particularly troubling about Obamacare is that it does not confront us up front and face to face; rather, it portends positive, consumer-focused change. The real impact, however, may very well be devastating to the current system. This chapter presents a number of problematic themes within the framework of Obamacare, as well a sampling of some problematic provisions. The list is not all-inclusive. Other chapters explore additional issues posed by Obamacare, exploring them in detail.

THE IMPOSING LENGTH OF THE PPACA

First off, Obamacare began with a bill that reached nearly 3,000 pages and resulted in a federal law that spans 906 pages with over 400,000 words! Multiply this by numerous cross-references to additional federal laws, including the (imposing in its own right) Internal Revenue Code. Also, the PPACA bestows upon the Secretary of HHS and other federal agencies the right to promulgate untold pages of regulations. Remember the Nancy Pelosi line about needing to pass the bill to see what's in it? You can memorize all 906 pages of the act and still not know what precisely it all means, since the details will be in the regs. Healthcare is extraordinarily complex, but that does not mean that effective reform needs to approach a half million words in volume, compounded immensely by potential volumes of regulations. Effective reform should be concise and, since it impacts all Americans, written in a manner that everyone can understand.

LACK OF BIPARTISAN SUPPORT

True healthcare reform should bring the two major political parties together, not further divide them. Obamacare has added another point of contention to an already volatile political atmosphere in America.

> Thirty-four Democrats in the House of Representatives voted against the PPACA. No Republican member of the Senate or House voted yes on the PPACA.

INDIVIDUAL MANDATE

Upheld as a tax by the Supreme Court in the *NFIB* case, the PPACA's individual mandate requires individuals to maintain minimum essential coverage or be subject to a penalty. The financial ramifications are soft in comparison to the cost of coverage. Beyond the monetary component, since the Supreme Court categorized the penalty for failure to maintain such coverage as a tax and thus a permissible exercise of congressional authority, being that Congress didn't specifically call this measure a "tax" but rather a penalty, this opens the door for future Congresses to levy additional taxes without being stung by the stigma attached to directly voting for a tax increase. Call it a "penalty" but structure it to function like a tax; avoid the wrath of voters because you didn't vote for a new tax, officially; and live (politically) to tax another day!

Moreover, practically speaking, the individual mandate will not accomplish that which it purports to accomplish. Obamacare's supporters posit that the individual mandate is designed to compel individuals to purchase coverage. In fact, Obamacare says, with respect to the individual mandate, "[t]he requirement *achieves* near-universal coverage by building upon and strengthening the private employer-based health insurance system"[1] (emphasis added). Note the language says "achieves," not "designed to achieve" or "is enacted with the intent to achieve" or any other reasonable language as we see in the text of many bills; rather, a firm statement regarding how the individual mandate will *achieve* near-universal coverage through the current third-party payor system. Even the majority opinion in *NFIB* recognized, "It may often be a reasonable financial decision to make the payment [the penalty/tax] rather than purchase insurance."[2]

The truth is the individual mandate is skewed to favor the penalty (or tax) as opposed to incenting the purchase of coverage. For the first year, the penalty for failure to comply with the individual mandate can be as low as $95. How this incents anyone to go out and purchase individual coverage is perplexing. Even after the first year, the flat-rate portion of the penalty increases only nominally to a graduated penalty amount of $695, subject to annual inflationary factor adjustment beyond 2016, and ultimately the percentage of income increases to 2.5 percent, subject to additional caps. With increasing premiums, how will the greater of $695 or 2.5 percent of income stand up as an incentive to maintain coverage? Many Americans may ultimately find themselves in a situation where they simply cannot afford to purchase coverage and lose 2.5 percent of their income because of it. So, while soft in comparison to the cost of coverage, the individual mandate can still be burdensome for many, particularly since it is effectively a government compulsion to act. The individual mandate's escalation with time may have been designed to ease the sting of this new tax.

EMPLOYER MANDATE

On its face, this sounds like a great requirement from the perspective of the average American worker. But not all jobs are the same. In America, certain positions have evolved for which the worker has some reasonable expectation of employment-based healthcare coverage, while others have not traditionally carried with them that expectation. Moreover, many such positions for which no expectation has existed may have paid a bit higher wage since they didn't carry with them other fringe benefits. These jobs have traditionally been associated with young, healthy individuals who are less concerned about healthcare coverage and more worried about how much money they will make as they save up to buy a car, motorcycle, trip to Europe, you name it. What will become of these jobs now that employers will be required to provide qualified healthcare coverage?

Moreover, the employer mandate is also unbalanced, in much the same way as the individual mandate, to almost always incent paying the tax as opposed to the cost of coverage (at least mathematically). And with the requirements for a qualified plan being subject to the affordability requirement (employee contributions to premium cannot exceed 9.5 percent of household income) and adequacy requirement (the health plan must pay 60 percent or more of covered expenses), not to mention the broad discretion the Secretary of HHS has to determine what specific benefits must be covered, many employers may not find it economically feasible to offer qualified coverage.

For instance, let's assume that a growing company, pre-Obamacare, became large enough and profitable enough to offer all employees healthcare coverage subject to a set contribution of premium by the employee. The market, and the success of the company, has historically dictated the feasibility of offering coverage and at what level. In the past, the employer may have offered coverage that today will not withstand the test of a qualified health plan under the PPACA. Under Obamacare, let's assume the same company starts to achieve the same level of success. This company might not be able to offer a qualified health plan. Instead of offering something, perhaps at a higher level of employee contribution to premiums, the employer will just pay the penalty. If the cost of providing a qualified plan proves too great, then we have a group of employees who are left without any employer contribution to coverage, an employer that is taxed because of it, and potentially a group of employees who will be taxed as individuals as well if they cannot otherwise afford coverage.

> In an unanticipated twist, labor unions began to oppose the employer mandate contained in Obamacare, citing the affordability and accessibility requirements as well as potential cuts to hours.[3]

Employers may also toy with other strategies to dodge the requirements of Obamacare, such as reducing hours to minimize the number of employees counted for the penalty, or by cutting their workforce to fall below the fifty full-time employee threshold.[4]

And we must not ignore the potential long-term impacts on US employers, who are already at a disadvantage competing in a global economy against foreign companies functioning without any of the checks in place on American companies, such as tight environmental restrictions and labor standards. The employer mandate adds yet another obstacle to competing globally and threatens to convert benefits to a simple cost-benefit analysis. The tax options will almost always win out if this happens.

MEDICAID EXPANSION

Let's premise this portion of this chapter on the fact that there is a social aspect of medicine. Medicine didn't evolve financed solely by those with healthcare coverage or the means to pay on their own. Let's face it: illness does not discriminate based upon the ability to pay, and neither has advancement in the field of medicine been the sole benefactor of those with means. But that doesn't mean that we should ditch the effective system we have in place today, instead of improving upon it, in order to prop up reliance upon government programs such as Medicaid.

Mankind does owe a duty to its fellow citizenry to render aid in times of need. This may be in the form of a mass response following a catastrophic event, or helping those who are down on their luck obtain, and pay for, necessary medical care until they get back on their feet. Obamacare's expansion of Medicaid does not accomplish this. Medicaid should be an option of last resort; we should not create a culture of governmental dependence when it comes to healthcare. Obamacare's drastic increase in Medicaid eligibility forms the first gentle step toward socialized medicine.

Moreover, the framers of the act attempted to force states to expand their Medicaid programs under the threat of loss of current funding for Medicaid programs. While the Supreme Court found this compulsion to be unconstitutional, the act's promulgators included a safety valve in the form of a financial inducement to states to expand their Medicaid programs. The massive infusion of federal dollars Obamacare promises the states if they expand their Medicaid programs may prove too tempting of a dangling carrot for many states not to grab.

> Health is a lifelong journey; healthcare is often an intermittent event. The migration from the current third-party payor system to an entitlement program means a shift away from the dual-incentive model whereby the insurer and the insured have an incentive to reduce overall healthcare costs by improving health and thus decreasing the frequency of healthcare.

OBAMACARE'S SINGULAR FOCUS

Another problematic component of Obamacare is the act's singular focus. This book is structured in the way that it is because it is imperative to understand that healthcare is everything and anything but singular. The woes that reside within the healthcare system, similarly, are multidisciplinary and not rooted in one, singular component of the healthcare arena. We have heard time and again about all the problems with healthcare in America. Yet, when it came time to do something about it, Congress chose not to take a multilevel approach to improve the current healthcare system but rather chose to highly regulate one component of many, the insurers. Can all of healthcare's woes be attributable to insurance companies? Certainly not! But insurers are the consummate bad guy by common perception, as chapter 7 points out, and they are fair game when it comes to regulation, or overregulation.

Effective reform would not single out insurers and overregulate them to the point of collapse as a way of bringing state-run socialized medicine in through the back door. Effective reform should focus, and with the minimal amount of governmental involvement necessary, on everything from the availability of practitioners and their cost of education to payment for services, and do so in a manner that enhances our current model instead of upsetting one component of the full universe of healthcare in America. Do you bulldoze a beautiful old home simply because a few windows need to be replaced and the floorboards creak? Or do you fix what is broken and preserve the beauty that does exist, striving to enhance it?

TAXES

Taxes. What more is there to say? Is there even a way to make this depressing subject more interesting? Perhaps in parody of an old nursery rhyme to the tune of "Twinkle Twinkle Little Star":

Twinkle twinkle, supposed healthcare star

How thou taxes near and far

A tax on the boss, a tax on each uncovered head

A tax on health plans and on the tanning bed

Twinkle twinkle, healthcare star

How thou taxes near and far

Enough said? Chapter 1, and in particular figure 1.3, elaborates on the taxes Obamacare imposes.

WAIVERS

Well-intentioned waivers are a great tool to offset unbending bureaucratic requirements and processes. However, waivers must be looked at with some level of skepticism when it comes to the PPACA because of the questions regarding the overall impact the act will have on the third-party payor system. Once again, the 906-page law cannot be used to gauge all of Obamacare's potential waivers due to the broad regulatory discretion the act affords various federal agencies. To say this should be concerning is an understatement.

CHAPTER 10

RECIPE FOR FINANCIAL DISASTER, AKA
THE REAL IMPACT OF OBAMACARE

This chapter will demonstrate the devastating long-term impact Obamacare will have on the current predominantly employment-based third-party payor system that forms the crux of healthcare in America today. It cannot be said for certain that this is by intentional design. But given the extraordinary amount of detail contained in this 906-page federal law, intent is not outside the realm of possibility. This chapter presents a theory that this pending destruction of the private healthcare insurance industry may have been intentional. Regardless of whether this was the desired end result of the act or whether this will simply be the unfortunate by-product of regulatory overstepping, the PPACA does threaten the integrity of the system that has provided care for the majority of Americans over the last eight decades. When the industry fails, we will have no choice but to accept the government-sponsored system that we have objected to vehemently.

Thus far in this book we have studied a brief history of the third-party payor system in America; a rundown of some (pre-PPACA) industry-accepted business practices employed by insurers to remain financially viable and profitable; an overview of the act itself; and a discussion as to why insurers are an easy target to blame for problems with America's healthcare system. Now it's time to parade the elephant out in its full glory and present what I like to call the PPACA's "recipe for financial disaster." As this chapter's title suggests, Obamacare cooks up this concoction that will ultimately bring to light the real impact of Obamacare. Unfortunately, you might not be able to stomach the result.

The most important thing to understand about Obamacare is that it mixes a noxious potion of doom for the healthcare industry. By attacking the healthcare insurance industry alone and without making any effective effort to rein in costs or streamline utilization, Obamacare sets up the demise of the system as we know it today. By focusing on certain industry practices that in themselves, without a full understanding of how or why they evolved, can seem harsh and callous, and knowing that by their very nature they are ripe for public criticism, Obamacare sets in motion the wheels of the cart that will ferry the healthcare industry to the abyss that is economic collapse due to (possibly willful) overregulation. An unbalanced employer mandate, a skewed individual mandate, guaranteed issue, and prohibitions against medical underwriting and preexisting condition exclusions, all enacted in the collective under Obamacare, create this recipe for disaster. Figure 10.1 illustrates the components of this looming crisis.

Figure 10.1

An Unbalanced Employer Mandate

The cost of the penalty will nearly always be less than the cost of coverage.

Tempts employers to pay the penalty instead of offering a costly qualified health plan.

- This means fewer individuals covered through work.
- This also means more dollars that might have otherwise gone to providing employee coverage go to the federal government in the form of tax payments.
- Less employment-based coverage means fewer individuals in the risk pool and less revenue for insurers.
- Fewer covered individuals and lower revenue means higher premiums.

A Skewed Individual Mandate

The penalty is low in comparison to the cost of coverage, which will escalate because of Obamacare (starting a vicious cycle).

All boils down to affordability, with the penalty often winning out.

- With guaranteed issue, no preexisting condition exclusions, and adjusted community rating, many young and healthy individuals may forego coverage.
- This also means more tax dollars for the government.
- Fewer young and healthy individuals in the risk pool means higher premiums.
- Those needing care will purchase coverage, meaning sicker individuals in the risk pool.
- More sick individuals depletes the viability of the risk pool.
- This all leads to higher premiums.

Guaranteed Issue

The direct requirement that insurers must accept all individuals and groups.

Practically speaking, the preexisting condition exclusion and the prohibition against medical underwriting provide for functional guaranteed issue as well.

Without reasonable safeguards, this flat-out prohibition forms an impediment to effective risk-pool management.

No Preexisting Condition Exclusions

Insurers cannot exclude preexisting conditions.

No reasonable safeguards exist as an exception to this prohibition.

Incents individuals to consider waiting until a need arises to purchase coverage.

- Not limited to life-saving or life-sustaining care.
- An individual with a degenerative hip could theoretically wait until he or she needs hip replacement surgery and then buy coverage.
- Transforms risk to loss.
- Depletes the risk pool.
- Results in major losses for insurers.
- Precipitates higher rates.

No Medical Underwriting

Everyone gets the plain gray rate.

Only slight permissible adjustments for age and smoking.

Increases the cost of coverage for the "good" risk population.

- The young and healthy balance out the risk pool.
- Adjusted community rating means that the young and healthy will pay more for coverage.
- Fewer good-risk insured means a depletion of the risk pool, which results in financial loss for insurers and higher premiums for consumers.

The way this will play out is that employers may not be able to afford to offer a qualified health plan, i.e., one that is affordable (not costing the employee more than 9.5 percent of household income), adequate (covering at least 60 percent of covered expenses), and containing all essential benefits required by the Secretary of HHS. Pre-Obamacare, such employers may have offered a benefits package and structure that they were comfortable with from a cost perspective, but now qualified plan requirements under the PPACA dictate the structure of the plan. This means fewer individuals covered through their job and more money put into the federal government's hands by way of taxes via the employer "penalty."

Individuals will face a tax if they do not carry coverage. But this tax, while meaningful to the individual who has to pay it, is very low in comparison to the cost of coverage. In fact, for 2014, this penalty may be as low as $95. Most health plans have an ER co-pay alone that is higher than $95. As we've already pointed out, despite the act's proclamation that "[t]he requirement achieves near-universal coverage by building upon and strengthening the private employer-based health insurance system,"[1] even the majority opinion in *NFIB* said, "It may often be a reasonable financial decision to make the payment [the penalty/tax] rather than purchase insurance."[2] Considering that preexisting condition exclusions cannot be applied and that with no medical underwriting, individuals will all receive the same premium rate with only a slight adjustment for age and tobacco use being permissible, the incentive, particularly for the young and healthy (who enhance the risk pool and allow insurance to function as insurance), to pay for coverage drops. As individuals choose to pay the penalty, yet even more money is funneled into the federal government.

With fewer individuals covered through work or individual plans, less money goes to fund care through the third-party payor system. Fewer individuals in the risk pool, and with a greater proportion of them being sick, means premiums increase. And thus we have a vicious cycle in place that may not be escapable.

There may be something much more sinister at work here than simply an unintended consequence, good intentions gone awry, or an unfortunate by-product of a consumer protection law. Obamacare's framers knew that Americans stand diametrically opposed to government-sponsored universal healthcare. We've all heard the horror stories about the quality of care, or simply the logistical nightmare of accessing care, in other nations functioning under universal coverage platforms. The long waits, the subpar quality—facing a similar outcome, we have said "no thank you" very loud and exceedingly clear. Obamacare's wise drafters knew this, so they did something that I must admit is ingenious. Rather than push a bill that proposes universal care, they instead attacked the less attractive aspects of the current industry, which were already ripe for criticism. (Remember healthcare's bad guy from chapter 7?) In short, Obamacare's authors targeted the unattractive practices within the insurance industry.

Consider the elements of the recipe for financial disaster as set forth in figure 10.1. Each enumerated component is a healthcare insurance practice that had been the subject of bad press in the past. Each regulatory result would appear, on its own, to benefit the consumer. But Obamacare's drafters didn't stop at the point at which most consumer protection laws end. Instead, they sailed well beyond effective lawmaking and regulated, restricted, mandated, taxed, and prohibited to the point that the insurance industry will suffer a fatal blow. For instance, the promulgators didn't impose a reasonable cap to preexisting condition limitations such as one month, or an imposition of the prohibition with respect to crucial care only; rather, they prohibited preexisting condition limitations altogether. And, as you will learn, Obamacare's drafters followed this process with numerous restrictions, each without an industry-preserving fail-safe, in a manner designed to destroy the entire system. They did this knowing full well that upon critical failure, the only option will be complete governmental intervention. This brilliant chess move will mean checkmate for the high-quality system that we enjoy today. Knowing universal care is a big no-no in the public's eye, Obamacare will bring about government-run universal care through the back door under the guise of public protection from insurers.

When will this occur? No one can say for certain. The insurance industry will fight back vehemently and expend millions upon millions of dollars to explore means of remaining viable and profitable, despite the draconian requirements Obamacare imposes. One thing remains certain: the resources expended to fight the inevitable industry collapse would be better spent enhancing our current American healthcare system as opposed to fighting its demise; all the more reason to continue to push for repeal.

It's also important to note that Section 1301 of the PPACA establishes the parameters, in a broad sense, of a qualified health plan. I say in a broad sense since, as you will see, the downstream requirements are subject to a tremendous amount of regulatory oversight and modification. Essentially, the Department of Health and Human Services has seemingly unlimited authority to modify the list of benefits that must be offered in order for a plan to meet the requirements of a qualified health benefits package pursuant to Section 1302 of the act. Figure 10.2 lists the ten "general categories" of an essential benefits

package; the details are left to the broad discretion of the
Secretary of HHS.

Figure 10.2

- Ambulatory patient services
- Emergency services
- Hospitalization
- Maternity and newborn care
- Mental health and substance use services, including
- behavioral health treatment
- Prescription drugs
- Rehabilitative and habilitative services and devices
- Laboratory services
- Preventive and wellness services and
  chronic disease management
- Pediatric services, including oral and vision care

A perfectly vague list, isn't it? The rest is left up to the
"Secretary [of HHS] to define the essential health benefits,"
and the Secretary of HHS has authority to "periodically
update the essential health benefits."[3] What this means is
that the insurance industry will need to contend with the
difficult requirements of Obamacare that formulate the
recipe for financial disaster, all the while contending with
the broad regulatory discretion the Secretary of HHS has
with respect to defining a qualified health plan through
regulatory-required benefits. The secretary can set the bar
high or low, thus influencing the cost of coverage
proportionately. This can be done to speed up or slow down
the industry's demise based upon public opinion and
awareness.

And let's not forget the tax on health plans that will fan
the fire while contributing yet even more dollars to the
federal government.

THE RUBY RED RUSE:
AN ILLUSTRATIVE EXAMPLE

Can the government intentionally overregulate the less attractive aspects of an industry with the real goal of destroying that very industry covertly? Is this not possible? Could it be that destruction of that which the people want to see preserved—via the guise of regulating the less attractive components of that very industry—forms the crux of Obamacare?

What better way to explain the theory of Obamacare's calculated attack on healthcare than by example. Let's assume, for illustrative purposes, that Obamacare is not a healthcare law at all. Rather, assume that the subject matter of Obamacare is agriculture, produce, specifically apples and grapefruit. Let's assume that everyone loves sweet, delicious apples and that the public preference for the juicy nectar of apples over the bitter and tart taste of grapefruit is clearly evident. Let's further assume that only a handful of people prefer grapefruit to apples but that members of that limited class of grapefruit enthusiasts become the powers that be in government. We'll call them the "Grapefruit Gang."

Not only does the Grapefruit Gang love grapefruit but they despise apples, hate them with a passion. The Grapefruit Gang winces at the very sight of an apple; they cannot even stand the fact that you enjoy them. The Grapefruit Gang so strongly prefers grapefruit that they want you to buy and eat only grapefruit. They want apples to go the way of the dodo bird. But, the Grapefruit Gang is wise and they know that if they outlaw apples (considering how much the population loves them) and mandate the buying of grapefruit (knowing that their bitter taste makes most people frown), they will surely be out of office come next election. The Grapefruit Gang also knows that apple lovers view the apple farmers, rightly so or not, as greedy fruit barons who keep access to apples low and prices high. So, the Grapefruit Gang devises a plan to end the production of all apples under the *guise* of making apples more readily available and of higher quality. The perfect "Ruby Red Ruse" if you will.

The Grapefruit Gang constructs a law that *appears* to make it easier and cheaper to buy apples, the PPACA (for this example only, our fictional "Peoples Protection Against Corrupt Apple-Growers" law, not to be confused with the actual Patient Protection and Affordable Care Act, of course). The gist of the PPACA requires farmers to charge the same price for apples regardless of the buyer's location, imposes a penalty whenever apples have too many spots on them, imposes another penalty for using any insecticide, requires that apples be delivered to market within two days of harvest, and mandates the removal of stems. These requirements "time in" as opposed to the switch being thrown day one. Sound familiar?

The Grapefruit Gang touts the PPACA as an apple-consumer protection law. For example, the Grapefruit Gang boasts that the PPACA requires apple growers to charge everyone the same price for apples, which will benefit more individuals than it will encumber. The spot tax and insecticide tax will ensure that clean, disease- and chemical-free apples will be delivered to market. The two days to market requirement will ensure freshness. And the no stem rule will save consumers from the arduous task of plucking those pesky stems off the now pristine apples. The result will be hoards of fresh, beautiful, clean, healthy apples available at an affordable price. Such a great law, the PPACA. I can't see why it didn't start all at once to ensure the full benefits to all apple consumers everywhere immediately instead of making them wait several years for all of the perks to kick in.

Are you buying this? Now, let's discuss what will *really happen* under the Grapefruit Gang's plan. At first, apple lovers may actually benefit from the PPACA. Some buyers will indeed see lower prices. Apples may begin to wear fewer of the unattractive blemishes that plagued them pre-PPACA. But before too long the apple growers will feel the sting. The sting will become painful, then infected, and finally necrotic. Then, there will be no apples in America . . . but don't fret, the government will step in. How could this happen, you may be asking?

Here's how it all plays out. Year one, the PPACA (the current fictional incarnation of it, that is) mandates that apple growers cannot charge consumers a thousand miles away from the farm more than they charge consumers right next door (guaranteed price). Apples must therefore be sold at the community apple rate to all consumers even though it costs the apple growers more to provide apples to consumers who live further away from the orchard. The handful of consumers who live near the farm will feel the pinch, but many buyers will see prices come down. The PPACA also mandates that apples must go from tree to market in less than two days in order to ensure freshness, thus increasing the farmers' cost to get apples to your table. Early on, many consumers may very well see some price reductions and slightly fresher apples, leading to the consumer misinterpretation that the PPACA is benefitting them.

Year two, through the PPACA, the Grapefruit Gang levies a delayed implementation "spot" tax on the apple growers. This tax is levied per apple if on average a grower's apples have more than three spots on them. At the same time the PPACA institutes a pesticide tax on every grower who uses pesticides to keep the number of spots low.

Sounds good, doesn't it? Puts the obligation on the farmers to find a way to produce the highest quality apples without resorting to chemicals. But either way you slice it, every apple grower is now seeing diminished profits. The fragile apple-grower's market is now an early frost away from demise. Smaller operations start growing other crops or leave farming altogether. The larger orchards downsize and struggle to make ends meet. Drought takes one of the last big growers; a late spring freeze seizes another.

Finally, in year three another requirement kicks in: all stems must be removed from apples prior to shipping or a penalty will be assessed. This wipes out the remainder of the apple growers. Many of them cut down their trees to sell for firewood. By year four there are *no* apples brought to market. People are starving. In comes the Grapefruit Gang peddling, you guessed it, grapefruit! The very grapefruit that no one wanted! Get used to the new slogan, "As American as grapefruit pie!"

How did this happen? The law sounded so good. The PPACA balanced the price of apples, required them to be taken to market quickly to ensure freshness, penalized farmers for selling apples with spots, created a disincentive to using chemical insecticides, and got rid of those damn stems. The PPACA was written to benefit apple consumers, or so it seemed. "It all sounded so good I didn't even understand why it didn't all kick in all at once. Oh, wait. I see . . ." The great Ruby Red Ruse!

Obamacare may perform the same result, the demise of the very system that Americans want to see preserved as a means of bringing in the government-sponsored universal care that no one wants. All accomplished under the guise of fixing the current employment-based third-party payor system. Once again, a Ruby Red Ruse.

IF OBAMACARE WILL HELP, WHY THE WAIT?

Be wary of anything that is supposed to benefit us in such a great manner but then must be "timed in" as opposed to taking effect all at once, day one. Be doubly wary when it times in *after the next election*. Great things do not need to wait. Great things cannot wait. Obamacare may be nothing more than a great Ruby Red Ruse.

> Many of Obamacare's core requirements go live on January 1, 2014, nearly four years after the PPACA was signed into law. The midway point was a crucial election year.

OBAMACARE AND HEALTHCARE INSURANCE IN AMERICA

Now back to the actual PPACA, the Patient Protection and Affordable Care Act, aka Obamacare. An unbalanced employer mandate, a skewed individual mandate, guaranteed issue, and prohibitions against medical underwriting and preexisting condition exclusions, all set forth in figure 10.1, comprise this recipe for disaster. All designed to "time in" on a delayed implementation schedule. Up front and on paper, they all look good to the healthcare consumer, don't they? But why the delay? And why no safety valves? Most importantly, what will the long-term impact be once all of Obamacare's requirements have timed in? If Obamacare really will improve healthcare in

America, why delay implementation of its core components? What was the intent of this structure? These are all questions we should be asking ourselves about Obamacare. The process itself raises as many issues as the substantive requirements.

> Even after the go-live date, additional delay occurs as evidenced by the time in of the full amount of the individual penalty.

It's easy to take issue with preexisting condition exclusions. At face value they seem cold and hard, unfair to the consumer. Critics present, in support of their discourse, the individual, a human face, who cannot obtain healthcare coverage due to a preexisting condition. Or the sad tale of a person in pain who cannot receive coverage for treatment under an existing policy since the underlying ailment is considered an excluded preexisting condition. Stories of high monthly premiums based upon medical underwriting add to the mix and further highlight these "heartless" insurance practices. Arguments against these practices garner a lot of public support. It's the weak and sick individual, the little guy, up against the mega-insurer with the pockets lined in gold. Like the spots on the apples in our Ruby Red Ruse example, it's not difficult to understand where public opinion falls on these specific, individual issues. What gets lost in the hoopla and rabble-rousing, however, is the cold, hard reality that many individuals are covered today, in an affordable manner, precisely *because* of these industry safeguards, not in spite of them. Moreover, harsh laws lead to drastic results. Look what happened to the apples in our Ruby Red Ruse example.

Let's not lose sight of the fact that insurance is, to put it quite simply, the buying and selling of risk. Certain industry safeguards have cropped up over the years to ameliorate some of that risk. Some are necessary evils, while others have gone too far. Obamacare does not attempt to separate the wheat from the chaff; rather, Obamacare burns the entire crop, applying a scorched earth policy to the best, albeit flawed, healthcare system in the world. To this effect, Obamacare does not simply attempt to quell problematic insurance practices. There are no safety nets, not even a fail-safe as simple as a one-month cap on preexisting condition exclusions (excepting out crucial, life-saving, or life-sustaining services) to discourage people from waiting until they need a knee replacement to buy insurance, as opposed to the all-out ban on them. There are no reasonable exceptions to the medical underwriting ban, apart from a permitted slight adjustment for smoking and age, to encourage people to live healthy lifestyles and receive a reduced premium for it. Obamacare was not written to simply cure the evils of the insurance industry, it was meant to destroy the industry under the guise of consumer protection. Once again, a great Ruby Red Ruse.

Certain industry safeguards work to help keep insurance affordable while incenting individuals to strive to obtain coverage either individually or through employment. These practices are not always pretty. And sometimes insurers push them too far. But Obamacare goes way too far in the other direction. Obamacare targets seemingly consumer-noxious industry practices without regard for the effects of the wholesale prohibition of those practices in conjunction with other problematic components of Obamacare. While certain of these practices could very well benefit from some level of reform, the outright prohibitions brought about by Obamacare threaten to tax the system's stability to the breaking point, and this will ultimately lead to full financial collapse. And this is all by design. Pick a point of contention and then overregulate it in a manner that appears to benefit its patrons, and destroy the whole system under the guise of consumer protection. A Ruby Red Ruse.

As stated, insurance is the transfer of risk in return for financial compensation. An individual, or more commonly an employer—either solely or, more likely, in conjunction with the individual—pays a certain amount of money each month in the form of a premium to an insurer. In return for this monthly premium, the insurer agrees to assume the risk from the individual, or in the case of an employer the risk that the employer has assumed from individual employees as a benefit in return for their agreeing to work for the employer. The actual risk is the financial liability for certain medical expenses should they arise. The uncertainty of illness or injury is what makes this "risk" as opposed to an easily projected loss or expense. For instance, if you knew you were going to break your leg in the next year and the injury will require surgery and rehab with a total cost of treatment being $35,000, then there is no risk; there is a known and actual loss set to occur within a set period in the future. No insurer would ever offer you a policy for $1,000 per month under this scenario since, due to the known future loss, the policy would be a $23,000 loser for the insurer. There simply is no risk under this scenario, only loss.

Insurers mitigate the risk of loss through the risk pool, utilizing industry safeguards such as preexisting condition exclusions and medical underwriting to enhance the viability of the risk pool. The more individuals in the risk pool, and the healthier they are, the more money there is to offset occurrences when the risk of loss converts to actual loss (illness or injury). This pooling also works to keep premiums down since the "good risk" individuals and groups are infused in with the "bad risk" members of the pool to curtail future losses.

The transfer of risk is really not all that different from gambling. The insured or the insured's employer, as the case may be, essentially bets money (the premium) with the insurance company that the insured will face illness and/or injury during the benefit period (one year) and that the amount to pay for treatment will exceed the amount of the wager (again, the premium). The insurance company takes the bet and is essentially wagering that the insured will not face such extensive illness and/or injury in excess of the amount of the wager. Just as with sports gambling, the house (the insurer in our current example) wins some and loses some. It is the sum of all wins and losses that matters, and in the insurance industry this sum is what determines financial viability and profit. Elements such as medical underwriting, preexisting condition exclusions, and open enrollment periods are akin to the vig in the gambling realm and work to establish an effective risk pool to ensure financial stability and profit.

What Obamacare has done is that it has stacked the odds in favor of the insured (in the short run, that is). And, it did not merely even the playing field, it loaded the dice. To consumers, this may sound like a great thing, but, as you will see, the long-term effect will be disastrous. The reasons why Obamacare's architects structured the law in this manner are not so visible on the surface. Drill down to the actual long-term consequences of the act, knowing the public disdain for a potential government-run universal program, and it becomes clear that Obamacare is a well-organized effort to seize control over the healthcare industry. Again, a Ruby Red Ruse. It wasn't merely a case of good intentions gone awry. Conveyed as an effort to simply reduce insurance company profits and increase consumer protections, which to the public at large sounds like a wonderful thing, the reality is that this recipe for disaster will strike a deathblow to the industry as we know it. Keep in mind that healthcare in America is only as healthy as the healthcare insurance industry. In the long haul, when the industry fails, the insured will suffer.

JOHN'S GARAGE:
A FRIGHTENING EXAMPLE

Now it's time for another example. Only this one doesn't involve apples and grapefruit, this one involves *you, your healthcare,* and *your future.* Consider, for instance, the following hypothetical involving John's Garage. A simple place with a quaint structure, John's Garage exists in theory on these pages but also exists in reality, albeit with minor changes in details, in small towns all across America. A little auto shop where hardworking people toil with their hands to make ends meet, John's Garage is the fictional embodiment of what life is like for many, an honest day of work for a paycheck. The purveyor is, of course, a man named John.

John's Garage hires Bill to work as the shop manager and pays Bill $95,000 per year. Not a bad salary, but six figures today is not what it was yesterday and this is still under that mark by five grand. Factor in a family and the value of this salary decreases even further. As an additional benefit, John's Garage commits to paying for 90 percent of Bill's healthcare coverage after six months of employment. John covers his employees under a small group plan, the likes of which were described in part 1. Bill therefore receives, as an employment benefit, healthcare coverage at only 10 percent out-of-pocket cost toward the premium. Moreover, Bill's 10 percent premium contribution falls toward the small group rate as opposed to purchasing a more expensive individual plan at full out-of-pocket cost. John's Garage purchases a policy to cover all full-time employees from ABC Health Insurance, Inc.

The financial risk—that is, the obligation to pay for medical care in the uncertain event that Bill, and/or his coworkers, should become sick or injured—has shifted to ABC in return for the monthly premium paid for by John's Garage, with Bill and his fellow employees contributing 10 percent of the total premium cost.

ABC may have employed one or more previously accepted (pre-PPACA) industry practices to better manage the risk it has assumed and thus offered John's Garage a better rate. These include medical underwriting and preexisting condition exclusions. These safeguards can at times have unfavorable consequences on an individual basis. At this point it is absolutely crucial to point out that the underlying theme of this writing, of the healthcare industry in general, is balancing the three often competing interests in healthcare: cost, quality, and access. When balancing (or perhaps juggling is the better descriptor) these three critical components, an individual cannot be the barometer by which the efficacy of the entire system is judged. When the individual is converted into such a barometer, then the stage is set for a potential industry meltdown.

Back to the industry practices. First, let's assume ABC employed medical underwriting with the small group, John's Garage. As described more fully in chapter 5, medical underwriting is the process by which insurers look at the health of, in this case, the employees of John's Garage and use such health information to establish an appropriate premium. In the present hypo, the rate was attractive enough for John to make a purchase. Medical underwriting can help or hurt the individual or group, based upon past medical history, lifestyle choices, and activities and behaviors that are healthy or unhealthy. Let's assume that the employees of John's Garage are an impeccably healthy lot. John encourages good health in his employees by prohibiting the use of tobacco on company property, offering healthy snacks to his employees, paying for gym memberships, and allowing employees extra time during lunch to work out or jog. John's Garage received a favorable rate from ABC, in part, because John's employees actively engage in behaviors designed to boost their own health, and their medical histories reflect this.

In contrast, let's consider the number one competitor of John's Garage, Sleazy Sal's Service and Sales. Cigarette smoke billows from the door at Sleazy Sal's. Sal orders pizza for lunch every other day and sets out bags of greasy snack foods for his workers. Gym memberships are not a perk of working at Sal's, but on Friday afternoons Sal treats his employees to beer, all they can drink. Sal's employees love him, obviously, but he is not doing their health any service. In fact, not only does Sal fail to encourage healthy living on any level but he actually contributes to a number of unhealthy behaviors on his employees' parts. And the results show it: high blood pressure is rampant among Sal's employees, two of Sal's workers are borderline diabetic, and Sal himself has had coronary artery bypass surgery.

Sal, much like John, also covers his employees under a group policy. Since ABC employs medical underwriting, however, Sleazy Sal's faces a much higher monthly premium than John's Garage. So much higher, in fact, that Sal can only offer, as an employment perk, to pay for 80 percent of the total premium, thus leaving his employees to contribute 20 percent out of their own pockets toward healthcare coverage. This is opposed to 10 percent at John's. Add to the equation that this additional 10 percent in cost sharing in the form of employee contribution to the premium is to a higher base rate due to medical underwriting, and the difference in out-of-pocket premium expenses for employees at Sal's is much greater than double the amount John's employees contribute.

To complicate the mix even further, to even be able to offer coverage to Sal's at a somewhat affordable rate, ABC has had to exclude coverage with respect to several preexisting conditions present among Sal and his employees. Therefore, Sal and his employees have to take the risk themselves regarding certain services until the preexisting condition exclusion period expires.

Comparing John's and Sal's, we see two very different sets of employees and thus two very different policies. John's employees enjoy lower rates based on their healthy lifestyle choices. John's newest employee, Bill, will soon receive healthcare coverage with an affordable personal contribution to the premium. Bill's percentage of contribution is low due to the health of the group, and the cost of the policy is also much more favorable, per employee, than if Bill had obtained individual coverage. Bill searched for a job that offered rich benefits knowing full well that if he waited until becoming sick to obtain coverage, imperative treatment might be excluded from coverage. Since Bill acquired coverage while healthy, he has no preexisting condition exclusions to worry about.

Sal's employees, on the other hand, are penalized for their unhealthy living. They face an increased percentage of out-of-pocket premium liability due to higher rates, which are through the roof because of the poor health of Sal's employees. Moreover, coverage for certain services is excluded because they pertain to preexisting conditions. In other words, the risk for an adverse health event for Sal's employees is high, and certain health conditions are already present. This increased risk, combined with the relative certainty of care for existing conditions, lead to higher premiums and coverage exclusions.

Enter Obamacare and the recipe for financial disaster as set forth in figure 10.1. Now, bear in mind that it is not the individual elements that spell doom but rather the sum of the individual parts, acting in unison, that comprise the recipe for disaster. From another perspective, certain elements in themselves are reform-worthy; however, Obamacare clearly creates a ticking time bomb set to explode sometime after January 1, 2014.

Let us revisit John's Garage post-Obamacare. Since John's Garage employs fewer than fifty employees, John is exempt from penalty (actually taxation) under Obamacare for *not* providing healthcare coverage for his employees. No big deal, right? John wasn't required to provide healthcare benefits before Obamacare and he still did, so why should that change now? Well, since Obamacare has also eliminated ABC's ability to medically underwrite and exclude preexisting conditions, John faces dramatic premium increases since ABC can no longer offer John an affordable rate based on the health of his employees, which likely had resulted from John's efforts to promote healthy living. Instead, ABC must employ adjusted community rating, which means that when establishing premiums the John's and Sal's of the world are lumped together with other demographically similar groups (with a slight adjustment for age and tobacco use only) to create one lifeless, gray rate for everyone. What's more, since ABC can no longer exclude preexisting conditions, that additional risk must also be written into all premium quotes so that the quasi-universal "community rate" becomes inflated in response. This means that not only do John and his employees fail to receive the benefit of a favorable rate in recognition of their healthy lifestyle choices, but they must also shoulder the expense of the additional risk created by all of the Sleazy Sals of the world. Sounds "universal," doesn't it? When John's accountant looks at the cost of coverage[4] in light of the newly increased rates as opposed to the tax credits John would receive for continuing to offer coverage, the news is not good for John and his employees. John reluctantly decides to drop coverage.

It's the perfect storm starting to come together here under Obamacare. Piecemeal reform or modification of certain industry safeguards would be one thing, but the drastic prohibitions and weak mandates devoid of any fail-safes, in the collective, combine to create a volatile and toxic nonsolution. Just considering the ban on preexisting condition exclusions combined with the prohibition against medical underwriting means that healthy individuals and groups will be punished since the same premium must be offered to the ardent health advocates as well as, say, those who live for the day. Not such a bad thing if you don't mind paying for the mistakes of others, but as the polls show,[5] most of us do not feel this way. In all reality this problematic combination actually equates to a "health disincentive." Think about it. If healthy employees and individuals can no longer reap the benefit of premium reductions in response to their healthy habits, might they be less inclined to continue to make the sacrifices that come with healthy living? Obamacare removes a valuable incentive for people to live healthy lifestyles. Is this the healthy carrying the burden of the sick, or the responsible footing the bill for the transgressions of the irresponsible? Just wait, there's more!

Back to our example. To Sal, on the other hand, the change is good! Since he was previously paying a very high premium due to the unhealthy habits of his entire staff, Sal included, his rate has now actually gone down slightly. The prohibition of preexisting condition exclusions and medical underwriting has benefitted Sal and his tawdry bunch. Sal continues to offer coverage and has now even been able to reward his reckless employees by reducing their monthly percentage of contribution to premiums to 10 percent, thanks in part to the tax credits he receives for continuing to offer coverage. No longer concerned about paying out of pocket for angioplasty, Sal gorges on all of the same vices that led to his poor health in the first place.

While Sal's employees have made out under Obamacare, John's employees are now faced with the difficult choice of purchasing expensive individual coverage or continuing on uninsured. In the past, the risk of continuing without coverage was relatively high based upon two criteria: (1) if an individual waited until illness set in to obtain coverage, coverage for that illness would be excluded; and (2) medical underwriting would result in a higher premium based, in part, upon that illness or perhaps even the inability to obtain coverage at all. In essence, it didn't pay to wait until becoming sick pre-Obamacare. If you did, the risk was great: higher premiums and you would have to pay out of pocket for the excluded illness if you could even get coverage at all. It made a lot of sense not to allow yourself to get into this predicament. In other words, insurance was allowed to function as "insurance" pre-Obamacare.

Under Obamacare, however, the tide has changed. As we have noted, the employer mandate is rather weak. In this case, the mandate is ineffective due to inapplicability since John's Garage employs fewer than fifty employees. Even when the employer mandate does apply, the structure of the mandate will certainly tempt employers to weigh the cost of providing coverage versus the cost of paying the penalty under Obamacare, and chances are good the less costly option will win out the majority of the time. By the way, the easiest way to get companies to stop doing something is to tell them they have to do it! I don't have any stats to back that statement up, but I doubt that you disagree!

Additionally, the individual mandate and its penalty (now deemed a tax, starting at the greater of $95 or 1 percent of taxable income, subject to an additional cap, in 2014), now applicable to Bob and his coworkers, is extraordinarily weak[6] as opposed to the cost of obtaining coverage. Moreover, assuming Bob and his wife have two children, with Bob's salary being at $95,000 per year, he is above the cap for any government subsidy toward coverage. Under the 2013 poverty guidelines,[7] a family of four could earn up to $94,200 (400 percent of federal level) and still receive a subsidy toward coverage.

1. Imagine being one of the families that fall just beyond the threshold when employers cease providing coverage and instead increase wages slightly to offset the drop in coverage! Since your employer can no longer afford to offer you insurance, he gives you a raise in good faith, which then makes you ineligible for a government subsidy! You have to be in the middle class to face this crisis.

2. Can the self-employed control their own Medicaid and subsidy eligibility by not taking on additional work if they are close to crossing over the next threshold? Will this hurt the economy?

This example illustrates just how easy it will be to make "just too much money" under Obamacare but not make enough to buy healthcare insurance. Bob and his fellow employees make the wise decision to simply pay the penalty rather than purchase insurance.

> Figure 13.4 illustrates the projected impact of Obamacare on rates and the resultant premium rate shock.

According to current reports, the average cost of coverage for a family of four for the year 2013 is $16,351.[8][9] Consider Bob's penalty for not obtaining coverage: for 2014 it is the greater of $95 or 1 percent of taxable income (1 percent of taxable income, multiplied by 2 to cover Bob and his wife, plus half the amount for each of Bob's minor children). The penalty for Bob's family is much less than the cost of coverage. With no medical underwriting or preexisting condition exclusions to contend with, Bob considers the less costly alternative of paying the penalty, waiting instead to purchase coverage if the need arises in the future. As one commentator has expressed it, John's employees can now "game the system," choosing to obtain and drop coverage as they need it.[10] In fact, the chief actuary at the Centers for Medicare and Medicaid Services acknowledged this in an April 22, 2010, report, stating the following with respect to individuals remaining without coverage after Obamacare takes full effect: "For the most part, these would be individuals with relatively low healthcare expenses for whom the individual or family insurance premium would be significantly in excess of any penalty and their anticipated health benefit value."[11] Or, in other words, the types of individuals who balance out the risk pool and make insurance work. Open enrollment periods can add some risk if the need for coverage arises between such periods, but given the difference in cost many "good risk" individuals and families may decide to take the chance.

As discussed above, it is very risky, pre-Obamacare, to choose to go without healthcare coverage. So how and why, in our example, did Obamacare change this? The answer is quite simple. For Bob and his coworkers, the cost of paying the penalty is far less than the cost to obtain coverage. In the past, had Bob chosen to continue uninsured and then became diagnosed with a severe illness that would require costly, protracted treatment, then Bob would be out of luck when it came to obtaining health insurance. Either Bob would have been deemed uninsurable, or treatment for his illness would have been excluded for some period of time due to a preexisting condition exclusion. Even if Bob could find an insurer to offer him a policy, if the policy were medically underwritten then the monthly premium would be astronomical. Pre-Obamacare, there is a real incentive for Bob to obtain coverage while still healthy. Once again, before Obamacare insurance was allowed to function as "insurance."

After passage of Obamacare, and more importantly after 2014, the incentive for Bob to purchase coverage in the present hypothetical scenario weakens. Under Obamacare his penalty for not obtaining coverage is lower than the price of a policy. The price tag for an adjusted community-rated policy for and after 2014, on the other hand, may be much greater than the $16,351 average for 2013. Even if Bob were to have a yearly checkup and perhaps go to the doc once for a sinus infection, then the cost of proceeding uninsured is still far less than the cost of purchasing coverage. Now, should Bob fall ill he can then purchase a policy that is guaranteed issue, meaning he cannot be turned down for coverage. His premium would be the same rate as for others in the same geographic area, with a slight adjustment for age and tobacco use being the only permissible demographic variances due to the prohibition on preexisting condition exclusions and mandated adjusted community rating. Since insurers cannot exclude preexisting conditions, the costly and protracted treatments will be covered. This means more people will wait until becoming sick to obtain coverage, thus reducing the size and efficacy of the risk pool with a greater portion of the truncated risk pool members being in poorer health.

Big deal, you might say. Let the big bad wolf pay for Bob's treatments. They *should* have to pay; they *shouldn't* be able to deny coverage. That's what health insurance is for, to pay medical bills. Well, what is the impact to the insurance company Bob obtains coverage with? Let's say Bob's treatment for the year totals $35,000 and his premium was $16,351 (the going 2013 rate). Clearly a losing situation for the insurer! Bob makes a full recovery, good for him, and decides not to renew his policy, as he can simply wait until he gets sick again and then purchase coverage. Now, as noted in chapter 7, insurers are the easy target. People love to complain about their insurance companies. But what happens when this continues, not just with Bob but with many like him, and the cumulative effect starts to break down the system that has covered *you* for years? What do you think will happen when insurers face less revenue to offset risk and struggle against more guaranteed loss? What happens when rates swell due to diminishing risk pools that contain a higher proportion of sicker individuals? What happens when the industry collapses and you are left uninsured?

> With Obamacare's Medicaid expansion and subsidy structure, the middle class will face the most uphill challenges of any category of healthcare consumer.

After 2014, when the recipe for financial disaster kicks in, there are several possible outcomes, none of which are desirable. Long term, the current system could go the way of the dinosaurs, with bankruptcy of the entire healthcare insurance industry being one possibility. Now before you cheer David's slaying of Goliath, ask yourself, who will pay your medical bills after the insurance industry has collapsed? Another more imminent possibility is that premiums will rise and since the natural course of supply and demand has been skewed by Obamacare, they will exceed price equilibrium and thus be unattainable for the majority of Americans. Individuals with lower incomes will benefit from Obamacare's subsidies, the funding of which has not been adequately estimated or planned for via Obamacare. The new class of uninsured, to which chapter 13 is dedicated in its entirety, will evolve: the working middle class. All the while the federal government will reap additional revenue in the form of penalties (taxes) from employers and individuals as the cost of coverage increases and employers drop coverage and individuals choose to "game the system."[12] This may be when the federal government steps in with its own plan, as was removed from Obamacare before passage. In the long haul we may see a shift to full socialized medicine.

The private sector may survive as a supplement to government care. We already see this today with Medicare Advantage Plans, which pick up the slack left behind by traditional Medicare. This means that we, as healthcare consumers, will be paying twice for our care. First, we will pay in the form of increased taxes to fund the government plan. And since the government (through the Secretary of HHS) will dictate what the plan will cover, numerous gaps will likely exist. Secondly, we will pay out of pocket for a third-party supplement to fill in these gaps.

It's easy to see it coming. The gray cloud is visible off in the distance and each day it draws nearer. The framers of Obamacare may have not only envisioned this demise of the American system but planned for it and set the wheels in motion to make it a reality. Why else would they have included a government option in the first pass of the bill? If the PPACA will work as proclaimed, what need would there be for a competing government option? If the PPACA "achieves near-universal coverage by building upon and strengthening the private employer-based health insurance system,"[13] then what was the motive behind the government option? How would the additional governmental expense be justified?

With respect to the limitations Obamacare places on insurers, Obamacare may look good to some on paper. However, the collective result of Obamacare will be the steady march to demise for the healthcare industry.

Think about Obamacare. The hard prohibitions, the ineffective mandates, the taxes. Think about the delayed implementation and the timing of implementation. Think about the long-term effects of all of Obamacare's requirements. Think about the cost. Once again, think about the taxes. Think about the Ruby Red Ruse and John's Garage. When Obamacare not only forces you into, but also compels you to finance, government-run universal care—in essence, makes you buy grapefruit—just remember, an apple a day keeps the doctor away.

> Insurance can be summed up as the transfer of risk, but Obamacare now puts the insurance industry at risk!

UPDATE!

On July 3, 2013, less than six months before full implementation of the PPACA's core requirements, including those components of the recipe for financial disaster, the Obama administration announced a one-year delay in implementing the employer mandate. Immediately, a number of concerns surface:

■ What is the significance of the timing involved?

■ How does this impact the recipe for financial disaster?

■ What is the real intent behind the delay?

Was this supposed to be viewed as an early Independence Day for American businesses struggling with the Obamacare dilemma? Or is this just another case of things not really being what they seem to be under the PPACA?

Senator Orrin Hatch was among the first officials to publicly note the "convenience" of delaying the mandate past the 2014 election.[14] The employer mandate incents a cost-benefit analysis with respect to choosing to offer coverage or pay the penalty, whether to expand the workforce or reduce to fewer than fifty full-time employees, whether or not to cut hours to less than thirty per week, whether to outsource, and a number of other elements that have a direct impact on US jobs. Delay beyond the next election removed the impact of the act on jobs from the equation. Moreover, delaying this problematic and controversial component of Obamacare fits like a hand in glove with the overall delayed implementation approach of the PPACA and offers further evidence of the act's true, underlying intent.

With respect to the employer mandate, the argument contained in the recipe for financial disaster was that the mandate would be ineffective because too great of a gap exists between the penalty and the cost of providing coverage. The mandate is a soft one, practically speaking that is. And while a bevy of arguments against this type of mandate in general exist (ranging from the further disadvantage it puts US companies in during this era of global competition to improperly incentivizing less employment), the truth remains that strictly and solely considering the recipe for financial disaster, the argument was one pertaining to the mandate's efficacy, not whether or not it is proper. Interesting, that this one limited check supposedly designed to prevent destruction of the healthcare insurance industry has now been abandoned for an additional year.

So what does this mean? It means that the recipe for financial disaster gets an immediate shot in the arm! Those employers who were considering offering coverage beginning January 1, 2014, get an immediate reprieve. Individuals will have the benefit of guaranteed issue and a relatively light individual penalty, which will fuel the problem of gaming the system by people who will wait until becoming sick to buy coverage and migrate in and out of the system based upon present-day needs as opposed to buying insurance in the more traditional sense. And isn't it interesting that the first year that the individual penalty rolls in at a lower rate than subsequent years? Only the healthcare insurance industry will suffer because of this delay of the employer mandate.

The real intent of the delay of the employer mandate seems to be consistent with the real intent of the act as a whole: the undermining of the current employment-based third-party payor system we have in place today in order to supplant it with socialized medicine dished out and run by the government. The actions taken to push off this particular component by another year only serve to bolster the theory raised in this book regarding the true intent of Obamacare being a full shift to socialized medicine. What will be next? Now that the mandate is publicly unpopular due to the negative impact it has on American jobs, delay would appear to be a give, but could it be a highly strategized and thought-out take? Could this be a brilliant chess move, planned out three or four moves in advance? Will others follow? What will we be left with? A shift from a completely one-sided law with very minimal industry safeguards in effect to an even more one-sided law with *no* industry safeguards.

Will the PPACA set the entire infrastructure of the third-party payor system into a downward spiral, a death spin, that could lead to a full-scale economic collapse of the healthcare industry and governmental intervention? Is it a variant of a poison pill, in this case injected into the insurance industry after eight decades of evolution and advances.

CHAPTER 11

LONG-TERM IMPACTS OF OBAMACARE

The shocking decision by the Supreme Court in the *NFIB* case dashed hopes that Obamacare would be stricken in its entirety. While additional cases are pending and certainly more legal arguments will be assailed against the act, none are likely to raise issues significant enough to warrant a Supreme Court overturn of the entire PPACA. After the *NFIB* decision and until November 6, 2012, many remained hopeful that the election results would yield the executive and legislative fruits necessary to craft repeal. However, with the results of the 2012 election ensuring the implementation of the most problematic components of Obamacare in 2014, we will have to live with the act for a while. It is unclear if any truly industry-devastating impacts will begin to show before the 2016 election. Regardless, the impacts will inevitably arise and be felt absent future repeal.

Figure 11.1 presents an overview of some of the more problematic long-term impacts Obamacare threatens.

Figure 11.1

The Uninsured

The massive Medicaid expansion virtually ensures that low-income individuals will always have coverage. The middle class will become the new face of the uninsured.

- The middle class will be taxed to pay for care for others.
- The shift will force the middle class to accept more and more expansion of government programs.

Jobs in America

The employer mandate hampers growth and incentivizes cuts and outsourcing.

- Employers may downsize or freeze growth to stay under the 50-employee mark.
- Businesses may cut hours to reduce the number of employees working 30 or more hours per week.
- Companies may outsource to avoid the obligation to provide healthcare coverage.
- Even employers that would have been willing to offer some level of healthcare coverage may instead choose to pay the penalty since they cannot afford to offer a qualified health plan under the act.

Quality and Access

New challenges to the government with the Medicaid expansion and subsidies.

- As we shift to a government-payment model, will there still be enough funds for federal research grants to continue on the path we are on?
- Without having a financial stake, what will incent Medicaid recipients to manage their health and choose cost-efficient options?
- How will overutilization be controlled?
- Long lines? Waiting lists? Delays to care?

The Economy

The ramifications of the PPACA extend beyond the healthcare industry.

- Will certain members of the middle class be willing to take lower paying jobs in order to be eligible for a subsidy, a higher level subsidy, or even Medicaid?
- Will the impact on jobs through middle class job changes for subsidy or Medicaid eligibility, quelled company growth in tune with the 50-employee rule, reduced hours because of the 30-hour rule, and additional outsourcing have a negative impact on our nation's economy?

THE UNINSURED

Obamacare has been portrayed as a solution to end America's problem of uninsured citizens. However, the act virtually ignores eight decades of private sector coverage and the countless numbers of individuals over the course of that time who received care because of the employment-based third-party payor system. For instance, in 2009, 66.7 percent of Americans were covered by private health insurance, most through employment-based benefits. During the same year, the percentage of uninsured was 15.4 percent.[1] In order to address the lower of these two figures, the PPACA imposed stringent requirements and prohibitions on the system that provided coverage for the majority of Americans. But Obamacare doesn't simply create a means to incent additional employment-based coverage and enact a framework to establish a temporary, needs-based solution for the uninsured; rather, Obamacare simply shifts the problem to the middle class. This result is so shocking that it is worthy of its own chapter, chapter 13. Based upon the recipe for financial disaster as explained in chapter 10 and the shift of uninsured to the middle class, Obamacare potentially threatens the loss of coverage for the 66.7 percent of Americans covered through private insurance in order to address the 15.4 percent who comprise the uninsured.

Obamacare will expand a culture of Medicaid dependency (remember, Obamacare expands Medicaid eligibility to 133 percent[2] of the federal poverty level). Entitlement programs, bluntly stated, do not foster wise healthcare decision making and appropriate utilization. Consider a comparison to a standard private insurance plan. Under private insurance, if you have cold-like symptoms, you are probably going to wait a few days to see if the symptoms start to subside before making a doctor's appointment. Why? Because you may have out-of-pocket liability to satisfy. You likely have a PCP co-pay so you have skin in the game, a financial incentive to make a wise healthcare decision. If you have Medicaid, you don't have a financial stake in this decision, certainly not to the extent as those with private insurance. There is no incentive to wait and see if what ails you is a cold or a sinus infection. So you run to the doctor and find out that you have cold that will run its course and you will feel fine, but you have already engaged two critical elements in the overall healthcare dilemma in America: cost, by virtue of an unnecessary appointment; and access, by accessing slim provider resources for an ailment that will clear up on its own.

By way of further comparison, individuals covered under an HDHP have even more financial interest in their healthcare decision making and their overall health, since they are further incented to obtain services in the most appropriate setting (perhaps a cheaper retail clinic or urgent care center as opposed to the emergency room). Once again, Medicaid members are not similarly incented to take a more active role in their own healthcare decision-making process. Entitlement to Medicaid, devoid of a personal financial stake, does nothing to promote better health, as it simply perpetuates the long-standing problem of treating healthcare as any other good or service. Why change the oil if someone else will pay for the repairs?

JOBS IN AMERICA

Obamacare will have an impact on jobs in America. Once again, this topic is so significant as to warrant its own chapter, chapter 12. Obamacare will not only impact whether or not your employer will offer you healthcare coverage but may impact the hours you work or whether you will even keep your job. In the worst-case scenario, Obamacare may even push American jobs overseas. Obamacare may stifle business growth by incenting businesses to stay below the fifty full-time employee mark in order to avoid the employee mandate; lead to cuts in hours to reduce the number of employees working thirty or more hours who would be counted for purposes of the employer mandate; and push American jobs overseas through outsourcing since those employees are not counted for purposes of the mandate. Chapter 12 delves into this issue in detail.

QUALITY AND ACCESS

Even if access to coverage for services does increase in theory (which arguably it will not), the act has not taken sufficient steps to make certain that adequate health *care* will be available. A greater number of covered individuals (assuming this for argument's sake, after a full shift to a single payor system) coupled with an unchecked physician shortage will mean less health *care* regardless of whether there is more healthcare *coverage*. If the PPACA can increase access, which the opposite is more likely in the short term with respect to coverage and in the long term with respect to true access to services, then it will do so with a disproportionate assault on quality since quality, along with true individual accountability, have been neglected. Regardless of how much of this startling outcome shows its face before the 2016 election, we must continue to march toward reform.

THE ECONOMY

The impact on jobs in America will directly touch our overall economy. Going a step further, for those employers who will choose to offer qualified coverage, how well will they be able to compete with those that choose to pay the penalty? As this plays out, the competitive financial edge gained by those companies that choose the penalty will set in motion a disturbing trend of fewer and fewer employers offering coverage. American companies will have yet another hurdle in the increasingly profound global economy where competition is already on an uneven playing field. One certainty about the employer mandate is that it equates to some required expense, either in the cost of providing a qualified plan or paying the penalty, which at best was a voluntary endeavor in the past, left to market forces. Now companies employing fifty or more full-time or full-time-equivalent employees will have some additional, and significant, required expense. There has to be a better way.

Strike while the economy is weak? It is important to point out the current economy and that of 2009 when Congress passed the PPACA. Would the PPACA have been pushed through if the economy had been in a more solid state? Think about it. In a strong economy, if an employer chooses to forego coverage and simply decides to pay the penalty, the employees might have more options. Other employers may offer similar pay for like work but also offer a qualified plan. This is something not likely to occur when far too many Americans are just hoping to keep the job they have or trying to find work. This hypothetical considering a strong economy is reminiscent of the economic factors in play during World War II (which gave rise to the employment-based third-party payor system we have today). In a strong economy, Obamacare would take longer to break down the healthcare insurance industry since competition would remain strong, thus incenting employers to offer a qualified plan as opposed to paying the penalty. If the true intent of Obamacare is to destroy the third-party payor system in order to replace it with a plain, gray, one-size-fits-all government plan, then there is no riper of a situation than a weak economy. When job cuts, downsizing, and outsourcing are the norm, there is little risk that your competitor will entice your employees away by offering a qualified plan when you have chosen to pay the penalty. Proponents of socialized medicine will make this very argument in support of their own position, however, by saying that healthcare in America is only as strong as the American economy and that this is precisely why we need socialized medicine. They will not address the deficiencies of socialized medicine, nor will they acknowledge a set of core truths about the American system: it has worked better than any other system in the world for over eighty years.

WHAT IS "LONG TERM"?

This chapter addresses some of the more problematic long-term impacts Obamacare may create. But when will this all occur? The recipe for disaster describes precisely *how* this may occur. How the shift of uninsured to the middle class will occur is also explained in this book, as are the ramifications the PPACA will have on American jobs. The vehicle by which the PPACA will build up dependence on government care while depleting the third-party payor system is relatively easy to understand. *When* will this occur is the question we should all be asking.

The answer, unfortunately, cannot be easily predicted. Insurers will fight vigorously to remain profitable and viable in the face of Obamacare's draconian requirements. It may be some time before a significant number of employers start to drop coverage either by restructuring to avoid the requirements of Obamacare or by simply choosing to pay the tax. But once the trend develops, this practice may roll like a snowball down a large hill, gathering jobs as it speeds out of control. The avalanche effect will be staggering. But when this will all occur is a mystery.

There are two constant themes throughout the PPACA that make it difficult to say when we will reach the point of no return. First, Obamacare is a system of delay. Although signed into law in 2010, the real meat of the act does not kick in until 2014. Even then, delay continues. The individual penalty gradually increases over several years, likely to ease the sting of the reality of the full tax implications it will create for many American families. The employer mandate has been pushed off another year. Obamacare was designed to take time and if the true intent is to replace the employment-based third-party payor system, then the act will achieve this by slowly chipping away at the foundation of the industry. When that final flake of concrete will fall is anyone's guess. The current system took eighty years to evolve, so its doom will not occur overnight. Secondly, the PPACA grants so much regulatory authority to federal agencies that timing can be controlled to some extent. Too much damage too soon? Pull back some regs and implement softer requirements. Moving too slowly? Enact tighter regulatory controls. In essence, these two factors create an element of controlled delay. What is more damaging, twenty or thirty bee stings over the course of a lifetime or twenty or thirty stings all at once?

Regardless of when the structure will fall, with the massive taxes Obamacare implements the federal government will be raking in additional tax dollars from individuals, employers, insurers, pharmaceutical and medical device companies, and others.

One can only wonder whether this was all intentional or not. I'll leave it to you to draw your own conclusion, but keep the following in mind as you consider the true intent of Obamacare:

- Hillary Clinton's attempts to lead America down the path of socialized medicine failed miserably roughly twenty years ago;

- Socialized medicine is a popular doctrine among a vocal few but receives strong public opposition;

- Obamacare times in;

- Not only does Obamacare time in, but the majority of the measures that will have a negative impact on the healthcare insurance industry do not time in until 2014;

- Between passage and the timing in of such critical measures, we had a crucial election in 2012;

- The employer mandate was set back one year consistent with the theme of delay;

- The delay of the employer mandate occurred just before the 2014 election;

- The PPACA enables broad federal agency regulatory authority;

- The federal government will feed off noncompliance via taxation; and

- Natural competition and savvy business practices will further delay the destruction of the healthcare insurance industry, even though this will simply prolong the inevitable.

It will take years, perhaps decades, to fully break the health insurance industry down and supplant it with a state-run single payor system but, intentional or not, Obamacare has set the train down the track. Is it possible that Obamacare implements a directed erosion of the American healthcare system?

> The single most important difference between the current American healthcare system and government-sponsored single payor healthcare is that with the latter, all positive components of competition have been stripped away. Devoid of market forces to incent cost efficiency and quality, the consumer is left with the healthcare that the government decides to offer. Moreover, the government utilizes additional taxes to fund care, which will leave the middle class with a disproportionate share of the bill.

Is this really what effective healthcare reform should look like? Is this an appropriate response to address the 15 or so percent of uninsured in America? Do you want the government to control your healthcare?

CHAPTER 12

OBAMACARE'S IMPACT ON JOBS IN AMERICA

Beginning January 1, 2014, the employer mandate—informally, the "play or pay" provision—of Obamacare will require employers with fifty or more full-time employees (or a mix of full-time and full-time-equivalent employees) to offer qualified health coverage to its full-time employees or pay a penalty in the form of a tax. Now, the nickname of play or pay is a bit of a misnomer since play usually means pay more. The play or pay provision establishes the rate of the tax to be levied in the event that an employer who is required to offer coverage for all full-time employees fails to do so. In almost all instances, considering the cost of providing coverage, the more economical action will be to pay the tax rather than to play by providing qualified coverage. The nuances of the employer mandate are discussed in chapters 1 and 9.

Companies started toying with options to dodge the requirements of Obamacare, even if it meant cutting hours and resultant pay, over a year before the full implementation date of January 1, 2014. It is inevitable that certain employers will choose to drop coverage altogether, choosing to pay the penalty (tax) because it is the more cost-effective option. Countless other tactics are being explored right now in order to avoid the requirements Obamacare imposes. As Obamacare times in, companies will undoubtedly explore an untold number of options, tediously pouring through the thousands of pages of federal laws searching for loopholes. An indeterminable amount of time, revenue, and resources will be spent on exploring avenues to avoid Obamacare altogether or to minimize expenditures under the act (once again, choosing to pay the penalty instead of offering a qualified plan).

One common practice before enactment of the PPACA was for employers (particularly small and mid-sized companies) to offer healthcare coverage, with the benefits of group rating, to employees but with higher levels of required employee contributions to premiums. Employers may have also offered benefit structures they could afford. These practices often allowed employers that would otherwise not be able to afford to offer employees coverage, and the individuals who would not otherwise be able to afford an individual plan, to meet on some middle ground. The PPACA restricts employee cost sharing to 9.5 percent of the employee's annual household income and, through details provided by the Secretary of HHS, requires benefit structures that may be unaffordable for some employers.

A perfectly logical question to ask is why would companies choose to avoid the employer mandate? How could it be considered good business to not provide healthcare coverage? How would it be worth the bad press that could result in opting to elaborately restructure in order to dodge the play or pay requirement or to pay the tax instead of providing coverage?

The first answer is that now employers are shielded from stigma, at least in part, for not offering coverage because they are forced to provide coverage or be taxed, just as we as individuals are now forced to carry coverage or be taxed. We are all in the same boat under Obamacare. Moreover, employers not only have to provide coverage but they have to offer a qualified plan that is also affordable and adequate, as established by the PPACA and the Secretary of HHS. They are no longer free to offer a plan that, perhaps not perfect, was affordable. Once again, we are all in the same boat as individuals are required to maintain qualified coverage or pay a penalty. And finally, considering the increasing prices of premiums based upon Obamacare's requirements, and the uncertain future growth of these premiums costs, as well as the fact that it may not be a case of an employer who does not wish to provide coverage but one who cannot afford to offer PPACA-approved coverage, the final element that comes into play is that the penalty is a tax. This renders the decision not as personal or corporate culture–based, but a dry tax consideration.

THE 50/30 RULE

The 50/30 rule sums up strategies employers may use to avoid or minimize their costs under Obamacare. Employers with fewer than fifty full-time or full-time-equivalent employees are exempt from the employer mandate. Also, in general, employees working fewer than thirty hours are not considered full time and are not counted for penalty purposes. Based upon business structure, growth, and other complex factors, some employers may choose to cap growth to stay below the fifty-employee mark. Others may downsize. Still others may reduce employee hours to fewer than thirty.

OUTSOURCED, THANKS TO OBAMACARE?

The IRS has stated that work performed outside the United States will not be counted for purposes of determining the fifty-employee threshold for Obamacare to apply. Outsourced, thanks to Obamacare? Frightening, isn't it? And let's be mindful that drastic efforts to evade Obamacare or the decision to drop coverage altogether and just pay the penalty will grow over time. Once the stigma and bad press conveyed upon the first few entities to take such measures has worn off, others will certainly follow. Inevitably, some people will see their job go overseas because of Obamacare; others will have their hours cut so as to not be covered as a full-time employee; and others will see the benefits they enjoy today go away because their employer has decided it is not cost effective to provide a qualified plan under Obamacare.

CHAPTER 13

AMERICA'S NEW "MIDDLE" CLASS OF UNINSURED

One of the more frightening potential impacts of Obamacare is that it will not reduce the number of uninsured in America but instead it will simply shift the problem to the middle class. Members of middle America may very well suffer a loss of the coverage they work hard for today, face skyrocketing individual rates that will make obtaining individual coverage unaffordable and a last resort, be hit with penalties for failure to carry coverage, and see their tax dollars pay for coverage for others. How will this all happen? The following effects of Obamacare blow the wind that will set sail the shift in uninsured on a direct course for the middle class:

- An unprecedented proliferation of Medicaid, unmanaged overutilization, and the resultant price tag;

- The recipe for financial disaster and its long-term negative impact on the healthcare insurance industry;

- Obamacare-based skyrocketing premiums; and

- Obamacare's domino effect on jobs and employment-based benefits

THE PROLIFERATION OF MEDICAID

First, the proliferation of Medicaid. Obamacare purports to push for more employment-based coverage to fill the gap between insured and uninsured through the private sector via the employer mandate. But the employer mandate is thoroughly unbalanced. Since the penalty may be far less than the cost of providing coverage, the mandate may ultimately lead many employers to drop coverage in favor of the penalty, or to simply reduce the number of positions or employee hours in order to avoid the mandate altogether. The truth about Obamacare is that it offers no guarantee that it will lower the total of uninsured Americans, thus no assurance that the problem of the uninsured will end. Nor does Obamacare establish an effective means of increasing the number of individuals covered under private insurance, particularly in the long run.

According to the US Census Bureau, in 2009 there were 46.3 million uninsured individuals in America. Also, in 2009, 66.7 percent of Americans were covered by private health insurance, the vast majority of whom enjoyed employment-based benefits.[1] Government programs covered 29 percent of those with coverage in 2009, with Medicaid comprising 14.1 percent of this number. These figures have been in a shift pattern ever since. Figure 13.1 illustrates these numbers for the years 2009 through 2011, thus showing the shift that is occurring toward rather than away from government programs.

Figure 13.1

Year	Uninsured (in millions)	Insured (in millions)	Private Sector	Government Program	Medicaid
2009	46.3	255.1	66.7%	29%	14.1%
2010	49.9	256.2	64%	31%	15.9%
2011	48.0	260.2	63.9%	32.2%	16.5%

Source: US Census Bureau, Highlights 2009, Highlights 2010, Highlights 2011.[2]

Figure 13.1 demonstrates that in the past few years the percentage of individuals covered by private sector insurance has been decreasing and the percentage of individuals covered under government programs has been increasing! This time frame spans the passage of Obamacare and the early implementation of the act. And, based upon the growing percentage of Medicaid recipients, this increasing government involvement in coverage cannot be chalked up solely to an aging populous (and thus more Medicare recipients).

Do you remember, for instance, the Obamacare requirement to cover dependents up to age twenty-six? That requirement timed in back in 2010, so the "before and after" status regarding this requirement is spanned by the data presented in Figure 13.1. That provision alone means more mandated coverage. But have we seen an increase in the percentage of individuals with private sector coverage? No. In fact, we have seen a further decrease in private sector coverage. Yet all the while the percentage of individuals covered under government programs has gone up. And here's the kicker: the percentage of individuals covered under Medicaid has risen each year as well. Remember, this three-year span from 2009 through 2011 is before Obamacare's extension of Medicaid eligibility to 133 percent[3] of the federal poverty level (which will occur in 2014). Just wait until then. Yes, we are becoming a Medicaid-dependent country.

> With the massive Medicaid expansion, some individuals may actually find themselves in a better position, strictly from a healthcare coverage perspective, if they are laid off. Of course no one would desire this, but factoring in unemployment compensation combined with the value of free healthcare, from a pure coverage standpoint this may be true for some. This can't be good for jobs or the economy.

In 2009 Obamacare was not the law of the land, and a shift was already occurring toward Medicaid and away from the private sector. Rather than reverse this shift and encourage more private coverage, Obamacare instead just throws gas on the fire and fans the flames with middle class tax dollars by increasing eligibility for Medicaid, although not as fully as intended based upon the Supreme Court's decision in *NFIB*. (Part of the decision found that the federal government cannot compel the states to expand their Medicaid program under the threat of loss of all federal funding for Medicaid.) Obamacare sets America on a course to become a nation with healthcare built on government dependence.

Beginning in 2014, Obamacare expands Medicaid eligibility to 133 percent[4] of the federal poverty level. Based upon the 2013 federal poverty guidelines,[5][6] figure 13.2 sets forth the eligibility for individuals up to a family of four.

Figure 13.2

Family Size	2013 Poverty Level	133%[7]	Medicaid Eligibility
1	$11,490	x 1.33	$15,281.70
2	$15,519	x 1.33	$20,640.27
3	$19,530	x 1.33	$25,974.90
4	$23,550	x 1.33	$31,321.50

Faced with either an insufficient subsidy or the prospect of no coverage at all, coupled with a personal penalty for not carrying healthcare coverage, this increase in Medicaid eligibility may incent some individuals to stay in low-paying jobs because of the "free" healthcare. Moreover, Obamacare fails to make Medicaid eligibility sufficiently contingent upon other crucial factors applicable to able-bodied individuals, such as a requirement to actively seek employment that includes qualified healthcare coverage. Beyond the issues associated with entitlement programs in general and their utter avoidance of creating incentives geared toward personal betterment and self-sufficiency, there is the obvious question of funding this massive government expansion. One can only speculate as to the negative long-term economic impact such a mandated stagnation and taxation model will have. And this "free" healthcare is not free at all; it is funded through federal tax dollars, which will inevitably come from some individuals who are uninsured but paying a new tax because they cannot afford coverage, with those proceeds funding care for others.

Increases in the number of Medicaid recipients and decreases in the number of insured covered through private insurance means fewer individuals being incentivized to manage their own healthcare. Overutilization by a growing Medicaid population may further negatively impact access.

THE RECIPE FOR FINANCIAL DISASTER

Now consider one important element, which, like the Medicaid expansion, will begin to come into play in 2014 as well: the devastating impact on the private sector that the recipe for financial disaster will have. Chapter 10 describes this deadly mix of time-delayed, industry-breaking charges set to inconspicuously cause the employment-based third-party payor system to implode. The recipe goes live January 1, 2014, so just wait until the 2014 Census Bureau results are out, and then 2015, 2016 . . . and so on.

Was Obamacare truly enacted to encourage more employment-based coverage? Or is it simply a ruse with the true intent being the migration of the US healthcare system to a socialized medicine platform? If, with only a handful of industry-impacting requirements in place before the conclusion of 2013, we have already seen a further decrease in private sector coverage and a corresponding increase in Medicaid, what will happen after the full recipe for financial disaster rains down on the industry beginning in 2014? Figure 13.3 outlines those certain industry-squashing requirements of the recipe for financial disaster as they relate to the shift in the uninsured to the middle class.

Figure 13.3

Recipe for Financial Disaster

An unbalanced employer mandate	What does the mandate do? It tempts employers to finds ways to evade Obamacare or to weigh the cost of providing coverage with the price tag of the penalty.
A skewed individual mandate	Just as with the employer mandate, the individual mandate will lead individuals to weigh the price of coverage against the amount of the tax.
Guaranteed issue	This will lead some healthy individuals to forego coverage and its cost, knowing that they cannot be turned down when they do need coverage in the future.
Prohibitions against medical underwriting	This will lead to an overall increase in rates, since adjustments for unhealthy behaviors will no longer be permissible.
Preexisting condition exclusions	This will also lead to rate increases as payors will adjust premium rates to account for healthy individuals staying out of the market, instead choosing to only obtain coverage after a need arises.

After the recipe for financial disaster times in, the negative impacts it will have on the industry and on rates will not peak and plateau; the situation will not level out in the long run. The industry will fight hard for survival, but once begun, the erosion will be hard to reverse. The destructive impact on premiums will grow as additional employers drop coverage, more individuals choose to continue without coverage or to game the system, and overall profit margins, already statutorily hampered by the medical loss ratio, shrink. Sounds like a vicious cycle, doesn't it?

SKYROCKETING PREMIUMS

Even before the recipe for financial disaster has commenced, projected rates already reflect the pending doom Obamacare will bring upon private health insurance. On May 13, 2013, the House Committee on Energy and Commerce released the devastating details regarding premium rate shock.[8] The committee concluded that Obamacare will in fact lead to a dramatic increase in premiums despite promises to make healthcare more affordable. The estimated premium rate increases, because of Obamacare, are truly astounding and are set forth in figure 13.4.

Figure 13.4

New plans for 2014	Expect a price tag that is a whopping 96% higher than pre-Obamacare rates!
Continuation of an existing plan	Even those keeping their current plan can expect a stifling increase of 73%!
What is the maximum expected increase?	The House committee has estimated that some folks can expect to pay 413% more!

Source: Rep. Fred Upton, "The Looming Premium Rate Shock."[5]

Obamacare has effectively overregulated the healthcare insurance industry to the point of unattainable coverage due to astronomical premium increases, all the product of the act's crippling requirements. The problem will compound over time as rates will continue to rise in an effort to combat increasing losses, fewer individuals covered under private insurance, and a depletion of the risk pool due to system gaming. Premium rate shock is the first symptom, the first measurable effect of the recipe for financial disaster. It is but a mere ripple, far from the core of Obamacare's full impact, which is yet to be felt.

Typically, the market sets the price, and this has held true in the insurance industry as well. It's a basic economic concept: you have supply and demand and somewhere 'tween the two shall meet and set the market price, or price equilibrium. But Obamacare manipulates the market with such excessive force that the entire process, and the market itself, becomes irreparably skewed, with the result being unattainable coverage. One need look no further than the recipe for financial disaster to see how Obamacare will obliterate pricing even further. Each component of the recipe amounts to an overregulation of an industry safeguard, under the guise of consumer protection, beyond any reasonable or rational level and without a single fail-safe. The projected premiums were already through the roof half a year before full implementation of the components of Obamacare that comprise the recipe for financial disaster, as evidenced by the House committee's report.

Why would Obamacare's supporters push a law that leads to such dramatic increases in premium rates if the intention is truly to entice more employment-based coverage? Or are things not as they are reported to be when it comes to the true intent of Obamacare? First comes premium rate shock. What next?

DROPPED COVERAGE

A number of employers have already considered dropping coverage altogether. Given the tremendous impact on premiums, as illustrated in figure 13.4, the prospect of losing your employment-based coverage is a real one and will likely grow as additional industry-shocking requirements take effect. If individual coverage has been mostly unaffordable even before Obamacare, with rate shock and other future premium increases looming in the distance, individual coverage will not remain a viable option in the future. Additional efforts to game the system and purchase a policy right before having surgery, only to drop coverage once fully recovered, will only have more of a devastating impact on the third-party system.

THE NEW FACE OF THE UNINSURED: THE WORKING MIDDLE CLASS

For individuals and families with income ranging from 133 to 400 percent of the federal poverty level, a premium assistance tax credit applies to limit the insured's premium contributions on a sliding scale. This works via a direct payment to the insurer whenever the individual purchases insurance on an exchange. The amount of contribution attributable to the individual after application of the premium assistance tax credit is limited to a percentage of the individual's income. It works like an advance on your return, with the credit applied as a direct payment to the third-party insurer. Under current guidelines,[10] a family of four can have income up to $94,200 and still receive a subsidy. This constitutes a further expansion of government spending and acts as a disincentive to employers to offer or continue to offer coverage since it softens the moral blows and potential bad press linked with not providing coverage. If an employer maintains a workforce of individuals who all perform a similar function and the average salary is within the range of eligibility for a premium assistance tax credit, then all such employees would be eligible for a tax credit that would limit their contribution to the premium. In a system that has traditionally seen the majority of insured receive coverage through employment, this structure conspicuously creates an individual incentive. In this scenario, the employer opts to pay the penalty since the bulk of individual employees are eligible for a subsidy. The employer then feeds into the federal system with additional tax payments and the individual obtains coverage by paying the difference between the plan cost and the subsidy (if needed or affordable) or pays the penalty, thus adding more fuel to the fire.

And while the premium assistance is labeled as a "tax credit" for the individual beneficiary, the funding for the assistance is based upon—you've got it—taxes paid by others.

First off, considering the skyrocketing rate increases the House Committee on Energy and Commerce has predicted, as outlined in figure 13.4, how affordable will coverage be even with a subsidy? And if you cannot be turned down for coverage when you need it, what incentive is there for healthy individuals to carry coverage and prevent further rate shock by becoming part of the risk pool? Apart from some open enrollment period limitations, there is very little incentive as compared to pre-PPACA times. An individual or family can very easily be above the cap for a subsidy and still have a very difficult time paying for coverage. If your employer, who once offered healthcare benefits, now faces increased premiums due to community rating and other strict Obamacare requirements, either directly or indirectly, and therefore determines that it will be cheaper to pay the penalty/tax (if one even applies), and you and your family of four earn $95,000 per year, then congratulations, *you* are the new and rising face of the uninsured in America.

Consider the ramifications of this. Four mouths to feed, clothe, and shelter. College funds to contribute to. Your family earnings are in the low nineties. You don't live an extravagant lifestyle by any means. You get by. You work for a small employer with fewer than fifty employees, so your employer is not required to offer coverage. Or, even if you work for a much larger company, the skyrocketing premium rates have forced your employer to cease providing healthcare benefits and instead pay the penalty. And if you are lucky, you may work for a benevolent employer who may even contribute a stipend toward coverage (but a far cry from the amount necessary to afford coverage and worse than your pre-Obamacare situation). You can't afford individual coverage and because of it you are now taxed. Your hard-earned money goes to fund care for able-bodied individuals who don't work while you are left uninsured and taxed.

The PPACA hasn't closed the gap between insured and uninsured; rather, it has simply shifted classes, with the new class of uninsured contributing toward the cost of coverage for those who are Medicaid- or subsidy-eligible while they themselves begin to lose coverage. The poor will have free or greatly reduced cost coverage and the middle class will no longer receive the benefits they worked hard to earn before Obamacare.

OBAMACARE'S CLASS SHIFT: MIDDLE CLASS FUELING OBAMACARE'S MEDICAID PROLIFERATION

So here is the scenario, based upon all the factors described in this chapter. Obamacare has led to unattainable coverage due to astronomical premium increases. Employers have ceased to offer coverage because of the premium increases. The private insurance industry has been suffering dramatically due to the recipe for financial disaster. The more the industry suffers, the higher premiums rise, the more employers drop coverage. A dangerous, vicious cycle. The US healthcare system as we know it is now set in a fatal death spin. All the while the poor, including the able-bodied unemployed who choose not to work, may benefit from the Medicaid expansion, and those on the lower end of the pay scale may benefit from subsidies, although those at the low end of the subsidy range may even find coverage to be unaffordable. All the while, employers who can no longer afford to offer coverage and remain economically viable, and while competing against foreign interests with inhumane business practices devoid of any worker protections whatsoever, increasingly fuel the government machine through taxes. You, the uninsured middle class, also fuel the government machine through taxes.

ENTITLEMENT DEPENDENCY

Yes, Obamacare does shift the problem of the uninsured to the working middle class who will foot the bill to cover others while they themselves lose coverage. But this will not be the case forever. There is an end in sight. It may take years, it may even take decades, but we will get there. Once there, we will be able to say, "We're here!" as we stare at the sign at the gate of—you guessed it—Universal Care Land! Once the middle class had been beaten, bruised, battered, penalized, taxed, and left out in the cold without healthcare coverage, the government will intervene and impose the government-sponsored single-payor system that no one wanted in the first place. Resistance will be futile at this point; there will be no other option. Too many Americans will be without healthcare coverage, the private sector insurance industry will be on the verge of collapse or completely in ruins, and there simply will be no other viable alternative at this point.

Figure 13.5 illustrates the full cycle of Obamacare.

Figure 13.5

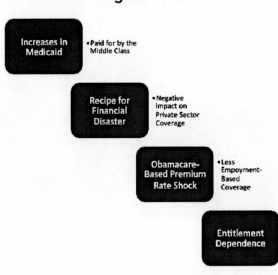

Figure 13.5 shows the current, imperfect, but effective employment-based third-party system falling down the proverbial stairs to entitlement dependency. Once the government takeover is complete and America has moved to a single-payor system, besides the obvious tax implications, what is to prevent the government from reducing the benefit structure to the point that it will be a mere shell of what it is today? Isn't it feasible that the government will control only limited core benefits and then turn again to the private market to sell supplement plans? We already see this today with Medicare. People may be at the mercy of the government and government-dictated care, pay dearly for it through taxes, and then have to go out and buy a private market supplement plan in order to receive the full spectrum of care they need.

> What will quality be like if we ultimately migrate to a single-payor system? Will government-mandated rates force many would-be physicians to choose other career paths? Will current practitioners choose to operate outside the box of insurance through paid membership programs for patients?

PART V

SALVAGING THE SYSTEM AND IMPROVING THE COST, QUALITY, AND ACCESS BALANCE

Unlike the scorched earth policy Obamacare applies to the American healthcare system, there is a better way. Solutions can be adopted to enhance the effective system in place today, reduce the number of uninsured in America, and meet the provider shortage head-on without a complete transformation to a government-run entitlement program fueled by taxes. But the PPACA is fatally flawed. Piecemeal reform of the act will not work. Truly effective healthcare reform can only arise on the heels of Obamacare's repeal.

CHAPTER 14

REPEAL AND REPLACE

With the Supreme Court decision in *National Federation of Independent Business v. Sebelius* coupled with the results of the 2012 election, Obamacare's position is solid at least for several years. The system's decline will begin to gather speed after January 1, 2014. But how much of this degradation will be visible on the surface before the 2016 election? Perhaps not that much. Obamacare is an elaborate structure, well thought out and designed to meticulously and inconspicuously eat away at the private sector system in place today. Even though the PPACA is excruciatingly detailed in some sections and regarding certain items, in countless other ways the act speaks in generalities and then bestows upon the Secretary of Health and Human Services nearly unchecked authority to regulate with as little or as much detail, as quickly or as relaxed, as the Secretary of HHS wishes. So, to predict how far into disrepair the system will fall before we cast votes for our next president is almost impossible; yet, on the surface all may appear deceptively calm. The underlying damage may be extensive and devastating but show only as nearly invisible cracks and fissures. Or, it may be full steam ahead, a blitzkrieg on the United States healthcare industry. Anything in between is a possibility. Figure 14.1 illustrates the broad spectrum of outcomes and the potential impact they will have on both the 2016 election and the likelihood of future repeal of the PPACA.

Figure 14.1

Scenario #1

- Effects are small and barely noticeable.
- Only a handful of employees have dropped coverage or manipulated their business practices and structures to avoid Obamacare costs.
- Individuals without coverage have chosen to game the system but the employment-based segment remains strong so the impact appears to be minimal.

Scenario #1 Result

- Possibly the worst-case scenario. This may create a false sense of security with Obamacare and lead to complacency among the voters. The damages are not visible so people fall under the false sense that the law is not all that bad.
- Mission accomplished? Frighteningly, perhaps. Unless we can stay focused on the true long-term impact Obamacare will have, it may not carry the significance it deserves into the next presidential election cycle. All the more reason to understand the recipe for financial disaster discussed in chapter 10.

Scenario #2

- Several high-profile employers have decided to no longer offer healthcare benefits and choose instead to pay the tax.
- Of the employers dropping coverage, the majority have raised salaries to help offset some of the cost to the employee to obtain coverage.
- Several US-based companies have outsourced production to foreign nations, keeping only a handful of employees in the US in order to avoid the shared responsibility requirement.
- A handful of high-profile employers have cut hours to reduce the number of full-time employees in order to offset some of the costs associated with Obamacare.
- Greater numbers of individuals without coverage means more people gaming the system. Negative impact is starting to be felt by the industry.

Scenario #2 Result

- More people will see that there is more to Obamacare than meets the eye. Nonetheless, the impact may still be slight, and on its face Obamacare may be perceived, falsely, as being less of a threat to our current system.
- It is imperative that we focus on the long-term impact Obamacare will have and view these negative occurrences not as the totality of Obamacare's unattractive side but as the tip of the iceberg.

Scenario #3

- Multiple high-profile employers have dropped healthcare benefits.
- No corresponding pay increases have occurred.
- Numerous manufacturing jobs have gone overseas in order for companies to avoid the requirements of Obamacare.
- More and more employers are hiring more part-time employees to reduce costs associated with Obamacare.
- Small business growth has been virtually stunted as employers strive to stay under the 50 full-time or full-time-equivalent threshold.
- The vast majority of individuals without coverage choose to game the system. This extends even to some individuals who receive a subsidy.
- With increased numbers of individuals covered under Medicaid and with less individual accountability, those individuals who do have coverage overutilize it.
- The provider shortage has not been countered. Medical school applicants' average GPAs and MCAT scores have dropped, with more of the stronger candidates choosing better paying fields with less future uncertainty.

Scenario #3 Result

- This will lead to more dissent, but will it be enough?
- Regardless of what big issues will be on the table for the 2016 election, Obamacare must remain at the top of the list.

In all likelihood, we will probably not see scenario #3 before the 2016 election. Obamacare appears to have been carefully and meticulously designed to accomplish its goal in a covert and clandestine manner. This is an extremely extensive law! It wasn't written overnight, and it wasn't designed to accomplish its mission overnight. It will be too early in 2016 for Obamacare to show its true colors, for there would still be time to feasibly repeal it.

Even scenario #2 is of questionable probability before 2016. The market will drive how far along the spectrum we end up, and it all may depend upon which big entity is first to drop coverage. If one or two huge employers take that leap and weather the bad press, others will certainly follow. Outsourcing is probably less likely, en masse, before the 2016 election due to the negative connotation attached to it. But remember, we have seen the outsourcing of plenty of US jobs with less financial incentive at stake. This may end up being a case of follow the leader, where one company outsources jobs and absorbs the negative press, soon to be followed by others. And central to the PPACA is a structure of delayed implementation, by statutory design, regulatory manipulation, and executive order. We have already seen the administration unilaterally, and without a congressional vote, choose to extend the employer mandate by one year.

Make no mistake about it: Obamacare will march steadily toward its destructive goal. That is why a focus on repeal must stay the course between now and 2016. If Election Day 2016 comes and goes and once again fails to bear the fruits necessary to upheave this act, then regardless of further deterioration and increasing dissatisfaction in the future, the likelihood of even returning to a shell of the system we enjoy today will be an unrealistic goal. And this should not be a politically divisive issue. Members of all political persuasions need to come together to eradicate this bad law and work together toward a common goal of improving the best healthcare in the world, not replacing it with socialized medicine. Ultimately we need a true bipartisan effort to address the real problems facing healthcare in an effective yet least obtrusive manner possible to improve care for all Americans. Healthcare must be addressed from the ground up, covering all facets from the delivery of care to personal accountability through payment.

Effective reform must balance cost, quality, and access by maximizing value in healthcare spending; incenting, not mandating, employers to provide coverage; compensating providers based upon the quality and appropriateness of care, not volume; creating effective individual consumer accountability measures across the board and without imposing a punishing tax on those who cannot afford coverage; establishing means of reducing healthcare providers' charges as well as reducing health insurance premiums; expanding coverage to reduce the number of uninsured; creating innovative programs to fund care, cover individuals during gap periods, and generally improve an already effective system as opposed to rewriting the book on healthcare insurance without improving care itself; holding tax-exempt nonprofits to their charitable mission; and avoiding a state of dependency where healthcare coverage becomes an entitlement paid for by all and without any individual accountability to access services in an appropriate manner.

We cannot roll over and die, figuratively or literally, when it comes to our healthcare!

CHAPTER 15

A BETTER WAY: ALTERNATIVE SOLUTIONS TO SOLVING THE HEALTHCARE CRISIS

Once again, cost, quality, and access are the three crucial components to consider when it comes to solving America's healthcare woes. The difficulty in striking a balance between these three often competing concepts—as well as the negative impacts of fraud, waste, and abuse, often willfully conducted in order to reap financial benefit—have been, and will continue to be under Obamacare, the scourge of healthcare. Inappropriate and overutilization contribute to the overall issues as well. So, knowing the issues, what can be done to improve healthcare in America?

PRESERVE THE AMERICAN SYSTEM

First and foremost, if we want to improve healthcare in America; if we want to more effectively manage costs; if we want to improve quality; if we want to ensure better access for all; if we want to even come close to striking that magical harmonious balance between these three competing factions, then we must first preserve the American system. Obamacare does not preserve the American healthcare system. Obamacare will destroy the American healthcare system and set the stage for wholesale replacement with government healthcare. This will mean more theoretical access but longer lines, reduced quality as funds are channeled into paying for more care as opposed to managing and improving health, and an explosion in costs. Obamacare will not simply take us back to step one, it will slingshot us back to the Stone Age. The first, and most important step to improving healthcare in America is the preservation of the American system, and the only way to ensure that is through repeal of the PPACA. We should then focus on what is right with healthcare in America as much as what is wrong with healthcare in America. True reform would enhance the current system and improve it to fill in the void left by the uninsured.

ATTACH STRINGENT REQUIREMENTS TO FEDERAL GRANT DOLLARS

Healthcare falls at the intersection of science and society, but that doesn't mean that socialized medicine works or is even the right thing to do. We are fortunate to have strong private sector involvement on the payor side, as this has preserved government funds for needs-based programs research. The National Institutes of Health (NIH), a division of HHS, awards over 80 percent[1][2] of its $30.9 billion annual budget through federal research grants each year. Your taxes fund these federal grants. Now, these grants are, with some exceptions, a great thing. Federal research grants play an enormous role in medical breakthroughs. They enable researchers to develop new treatments and find new cures. I dread the position we would be in had it not been for these research dollars throughout the years. What has worked in America—and compared to other nations' healthcare systems, the US system does work—is a focus of government funding toward research, with the private sector predominantly managing the payment for services. The government cannot drastically expand its role to become the single payor for healthcare services without sacrificing quality and increasing each American's out-of-pocket contribution through massive tax increases. That's the true and simple reality of it all. What better hook, then, to influence the status of healthcare in America than federal grant dollars?

The concept is quite simple: attach appropriate conditions to federal grant awards. For instance, if a large university owns or otherwise has an affiliate health system, then appropriate conditions and requirements can be attached to the health system by virtue of the grant award. In other words, if you are going to accept the people's money, then you have to give something back to the people who funded the grant. And while the opportunities are endless, caution should be exercised to avoid overregulation. Obamacare is teaching us about the ills of overregulation!

As an aside, it is the private sector's role and involvement as the primary payor of healthcare services over the last eight decades that has permitted the federal healthcare grant program to be such a success. How can we expect the government to fund not only research and development through the current grant program and at the same time take on more responsibilities as a payor, first through a massive Medicaid expansion and ultimately through a full migration to a government-based single-payor system? The only way to do it is to, guess what, increase taxes! The only other alternative is to reduce grant awards. Either way, we all lose. The government simply cannot take on the dual role of paying for research and paying for care without something breaking. That something may be our bank accounts.

CURTAIL AGGRESSIVE NONPROFITS

The majority of hospitals in America are organized as not-for-profit legal entities. Many of these, in increasing numbers each year, are large, academic medical centers. Disappearing is the small, lone, charitable community hospital. They have been devoured over the past couple decades by the emerging university-affiliated academic medical center. While many of these giants enjoy tax-exempt status, more and more we are seeing these huge corporate entities behaving not like charitable, community, asset-based nonprofits but as cutthroat megacorporations. More and more of these systems represent the proverbial wolf in sheep's clothing. The reason that this is permitted to occur is that many of the laws regarding nonprofit status are vague, ambiguous, and far too easy to satisfy. Nonprofits should be required to behave as nonprofits, and certain conditions can be written into the laws that govern nonprofit and tax-exempt status that can also be applied to the federal grant structure.

END THE PROVIDER SHORTAGE

As a lawyer, I can tell you that in America today, we have too many lawyers! All jokes aside, the practical reality is that our lawyer bucket is full and our physician bucket is not. We need to train more healthcare providers, plain and simple. Why not expand innovative opportunities to cut the shortage off at the pass, such as a three-year, PCP-only, medical school track to reduce the physician shortage?[3] Not only will this shave 25 percent off the cost associated with producing much-needed primary care physicians, but it is supported by research as a feasible track to training the type of doctor most in demand today.

Shortage equals higher costs. Medical school matriculation rates have been kept artificially low.[4] The purported reason has been to avoid a surplus. Common sense tells us the real answer: fewer doctors to go around means they command a higher price. Just compare average physician salaries with the average salaries of other learned professionals and the intent shows its obvious face.

Curtail the physician shortage and you accomplish two significant goals. First, you reduce costs and secondly, you increase access. The three-year medical school PCP track helps accomplish this. The shorter track will lead to more PCPs, as the three-year cycle means a new crop of PCPs will graduate every three years instead of four, with an entire year of education cost shaved off.

It is interesting that this option was not explored until other mid-level professionals successfully lobbied for expanded practice roles. Advanced practice nurses have been taking on more traditional PCP roles with much shorter and cheaper online training. Expansion of mid-level provider roles, particularly nurse practitioners, provides evidence that less time in the classroom can help alleviate the practitioner shortage without sacrificing provider efficacy. It is time for the medical community to acknowledge that far too many qualified applicants are being turned away and the spaces that those would-be matriculants leave open are being filled by non-physicians serving in roles with ever-increasing scopes of practice and autonomy. More three-year medical school programs would be a solid first step.

EFFECTIVE INSURANCE REFORM

Please note, the subheading above says "effective." This, unfortunately, is not a concept effectuated by the PPACA.

Yes, there is room for reform, but not the crippling overregulation brought on through Obamacare. Effective insurance reform curtails problematic practices and improves outcomes for members without bankrupting the entire insurance industry and without inefficient and costly overregulation. For instance, Obamacare imposes a flat-out restriction on preexisting condition exclusions. Coupled with other problematic provisions of the PPACA, this unwavering prohibition threatens to transform risk to loss, thus striking a blow to the core of the healthcare insurance industry.

Are there bad actors in the insurance industry that have exploited this component of insurance over the years? Absolutely. Is this something that needs to be addressed? Yes; in fact most states had already addressed preexisting condition exclusions by imposing limits on the practice. But is it okay for an individual with a bad knee, and who knows it, to choose to go without insurance for years because it is to his financial benefit to do so and because he knows the knee has not deteriorated to the point where surgical replacement is warranted? The type of flat-out prohibition Obamacare has created, without reasonable fail-safes, allows the person to pocket additional money for years and then buy a policy at the same rate others had been paying all along when his knee finally needs surgery. Even if you can get past the inherent unfairness prevalent in this hypothetical, you cannot ignore the cumulative effect of this very type of exploitation, multiplied by the numerous other PPACA insurance industry death traps disguised as consumer protections, and the ultimate impact this will have on the insurance industry.

Prohibiting policy cancellation based on a technical issue is reasonable. So, too, is a requirement to provide notice of termination with a cure period for nonpayment. Mandating a solid verification process to be part of open enrollment would be reasonable, as would a ninety-day cap on preexisting condition exclusions. It's not hard to figure out which practices in the healthcare insurance arena need to be curtailed, nor is it difficult to understand the need to avoid draconian, industry-breaking rules, regulations, and penalties. A cooperative, bipartisan group could accomplish this in relatively short order. The industry would have no defensible gripe against these regulations, and gone would be the individual horror stories of a person losing coverage and not being able to obtain necessary care because of a technicality-based policy cancellation.

Unfortunately, Obamacare's promulgators used these individual horror stories to fuel public discord for all insurers, based on the practices of the unscrupulous few, and then overregulated the healthcare insurance industry to its pending demise.

INCENTIVES FOR EMPLOYMENT-BASED COVERAGE

Mandated employer coverage, by way of Obamacare, creates risks that go beyond the healthcare industry. Competition in business is now global. US companies struggle against foreign competitors that engage in business practices that would not only be illegal in the United States but are more than unethical, and at times even immoral. Mandated coverage just piles on additional weight to an already shaky structure. Effective reform incentivizes employer-based coverage while giving employers the ability to select or offer plans that strike a balance between what their employees need and what the employer can afford to offer. Obamacare does offer some tax breaks for small businesses, but the issues caused by the employer mandate far surpass any benefit of this singular component. Why shouldn't an incentive be extended to large employers as well? And why wasn't Obamacare structured this way? Because tax credits as an incentive to offering coverage ultimately means less tax dollars received by the government when the incentive does its job, whereas Obamacare simply adds an additional tax, on top of what is already due, for noncompliance with the mandate.

> Mandates don't work, incentives do!

KEEP MEDICAID NEEDS BASED

Medicaid should not be a long-term option. Medicaid should be preserved for low-income citizens who are disabled, pregnant, or otherwise have a true need. Medicaid should not be transformed to a long-term solution based solely on income. No able-bodied adult should be allowed to spend a lifetime on Medicaid that is paid for by people who themselves may not have coverage. A reasonable expansion, as funds permit, would be acceptable provided it doesn't add additional and unreasonable tax consequences. Perhaps short-term coverage, or limited coverage after job loss, in a similar structure to unemployment compensation, could work, but transforming Medicaid to a permanent program for many is not effective healthcare reform.

The suggestions presented in this chapter in no manner constitute the full spectrum of options to more effectively improve the American healthcare system. These are but a few options of countless many that can lead to a broad improvement in the entire healthcare industry in America. Figure 15.1 illustrates how effective reform should be built.

Figure 15.1

Effective reform should be concise and easily understood.	▪ A 906-page law is far too long. ▪ The average American should be able to read the law and understand most of it. ▪ There should be no hidden agenda. ▪ Regulatory agency authority should be kept to a minimum and within a set of clearly defined parameters.
Effective reform should cover the full spectrum of healthcare in America.	▪ Patients ▪ Providers ▪ Payors
Incentives work, mandates don't.	▪ Incent, don't force, employers to extend coverage. ▪ Incent, don't force, individuals to strive to obtain coverage.
Keep taxes to a minimum.	▪ Less taxes means less government involvement. ▪ Extend tax breaks instead of new taxes to keep coverage employment based.
Enhance, don't replace, the current system.	▪ Fix what is broken without breaking the system. ▪ Keep government involvement as a payor to a minimum.

CONCLUSION

If subprime mortgages and an economy focused primarily on buying and selling debt were the precursor to the 2008 economic collapse, then the PPACA is certainly the precursor to the downfall of the healthcare industry. The difference is we now have the luxury, or perhaps the misfortune, of being able to see it coming. The government option, scrapped at the last minute, would have created the takeover entity poised to relinquish all free market components from healthcare in America after the private sector fall. Even with the government option off the table, the massive Medicaid expansion Obamacare creates will form a formidable step toward socialized medicine. If the government runs healthcare, the government generates revenue from healthcare. Increase taxes to meet rising costs, then unilaterally set the rates to retain profit. Quality suffers, actual access is depleted, and it costs us all more in taxes.

The multifarious taxes Obamacare creates will have a pronounced impact not only on the private healthcare insurance sector but ultimately on the entire healthcare industry and the economy as a whole. Taxes on individuals, businesses, Cadillac health plans, insurers, high earners, and pharmaceutical and medical device manufacturers and importers, to name a few, will bring about a massive infusion of tax dollars to the federal government. These tax dollars will fund the conversion of Medicaid as a predominantly needs-based last resort today to a cut-and-dry income-based entitlement program.

Many businesses will be forced to offer qualified health plans, the details of which will be dictated by the Secretary of HHS. Businesses may even be forced to provide coverage for services that they object to on religious grounds. Some businesses that would have otherwise offered employees coverage options that they could afford yesterday will simply pay the tax instead of the highly inflated cost of coverage Obamacare will create. This will deplete the model that has provided the majority of coverage for Americans over the past eight decades.

The individual mandate will mean, for many Americans, that they will be forced to purchase something that they cannot afford. While the framers of Obamacare, and the majority opinion in the *NFIB* case, liken this too a reverse scenario (where there is imposed a tax and a credit for that tax for individuals who have qualified coverage), the practical reality and the end result means you are forced to obtain something you cannot afford, with the penalty (while still significant) being far less than the price of a policy.

The Supreme Court decision in the *NFIB* case means that Congress is authorized to require individuals to engage in some behavior or take some action, a deviation from the historical framework of legislation being limited to regulating some action that otherwise occurs. This is accomplished by imposing a tax for failure to take the action Congress wants to compel and then offering a tax credit for compliance. Furthermore, Congress can call it a "penalty" but structure the penalty to act as a tax and thus impose an entirely new tax without having to cast a vote in favor of an additional tax.

Under Obamacare, unbending healthcare insurance industry prohibitions and regulatory control step far beyond reasonable oversight to prevent unscrupulous practices. This will hamper the time-tested industry intricacies that enable insurance to function as insurance as opposed to guaranteed loss. The industry will suffer and premium prices will rise as the third-party model begins to fail, thus fueling the fire that will ultimately engulf the employment-based third-party payor system. All the while, individuals and families will see more of their hard-earned dollars forfeited to the government through this mandate-based tax/penalty structure, which will then be used to fund care for others while they themselves go without healthcare coverage. With Medicaid guaranteed based upon income, the middle class will become the new class of uninsured in America. As the middle class loses coverage, all the while having contributed to the government model in waiting, the government will intervene with the public-sector option pulled from the PPACA bill at the last moment. Left without choice, and with the private-sector model in ruins, the middle class will have no option but to grudgingly accept universal care.

All free market influences that enhance quality in the face of demand will have been lost. Nothing will act as a check on the government adding or raising taxes to fund the only option on the table, socialized medicine. We will ultimately pay more as individuals and since the government will be the only payor, the market will not influence rates in a fair manner. Government rates will mean a drop in quality, and with third-party system-imposed measures designed to incent individual accountability gone, overutilization will result. This will mean more coverage but less actual access as long lines and waiting lists form. It will take weeks to see your doctor, while curable cancers metastasize and shortcuts are taken in the interest of time. There will be no improvement in cost to the consumer as taxes increase, with the middle class and high earners paying a disproportionate share, only to receive less quality and even worse access. Duplicative payment may be the norm as private insurance has survived on a limited basis to offer supplemental plans to fill the many gaps left by the government plan. This is the future of healthcare in America under the PPACA.

Should Obamacare be left to stand unaltered without allowing a ray of light to begin to shine with hope for an even better healthcare system, the outlook will be bleak. Repeal of the Patient Protection and Affordable Care Act is key. We must start from scratch with a truly effective reform effort. We must look at our current system and note where the strengths lie and bolster, not hamper and replace them. We must find the inefficiencies and gaps and correct them. Effective change must arise from the ashes of the PPACA and share support from both political parties. With some innovative solutions, America can reign as the world's undisputed healthcare leader.

Be sure to keep current by checking in at www.endobamacare.net for news and updates regarding Obamacare.

REFERENCES

Introduction

3. "Constitution of the United States Questions and Answers." http://www.archives.gov/exhibits/charters/constitution_q_and_a.html

4. The Patient Protection and Affordable Care Act will referred to throughout as the "PPACA," "Obamacare," or generically as "the act." References to the PPACA in bill form will be distinguished where applicable.

5. Payor, a nonstandard spelling of payer, is a legal term that refers to "the party who must make payment on a promissory note" (source: Law.com).

6. Jordan Fabian, "Pelosi: Public option will not be in health bill despite liberal efforts to revive it," The Hill. http://thehill.com/blogs/blog-briefing-room/news/86447-pelosi-public-option-will-not-be-in-health-bill

7. Amanda Cochran, "CBS News poll finds more Americans than ever want Obamacare repealed," CBS News. http://www.cbsnews.com/8301-505267_162-57595225/cbs-news-poll-finds-more-americans-than-ever-want-obamacare-repealed/

8. "Health Care Law: 47% Think Health Care System Will Worsen Over Next Two Years," Rasmussen Reports. http://www.rasmussenreports.com/public_content/politics/current_events/healthcare/health_care_law

9. Adam Taylor and Samuel Blackstone, "These are the 36 Countries That Have Better Healthcare Systems Than the US," Business Insider International. http://www.businessinsider.com/best-healthcare-systems-in-the-world-2012-6?op=1

10. Rasmussen Reports, "47% Think Health Care System Will Worsen."

11. National Federation of Independent Business v. Sebelius, 567 US _____ (2012)

Chapter 1

1. Mike Ward, "'Obamacare' contains money for Texas prisoners' health care," Statesman.com. http ://www.statesman.com/news/news/state-regional-govt-politics /obamacare-contains-money-for-texas-prisoners-healt/nRgy7/

2. Figures 1.1 and 1.2 describe PPACA provisions using industry terms. Please refer to the glossary in chapter 5 for additional information regarding these terms.

3. This figure could be increased to 138 percent based upon use of Modified Adjusted Gross Income as established by the PPACA.

4. "CEO of Papa John's says employees' hours will likely be cut due to ObamaCare," Fox News. http://www.foxnews.com/us/2012/11/11/ceo-papa-john-says-employees-hours-will-likely-be-cut-due-to-obamacare/

5. "Questions and Answers on Employer Shared Responsibility Provisions Under the Affordable Care Act," Internal Revenue Service. http ://www.irs.gov/uac/Newsroom/Questions-and-Answers-on-Employer -Shared-Responsibility-Provisions-Under-the-Affordable-Care-Act

6. "Highlights 2011," US Census Bureau. http://www.census.gov/hhes/www/hlthins/data/incpovhlth/2011/highlights.html

7. "Highlights 2009," US Census Bureau. http://www.census.gov/hhes/www/hlthins/data/incpovhlth/2011/highlights.html

8. "The Patient Protection and Affordable Care Act," Government Printing Office. http://www.census.gov/hhes/www/hlthins/data/incpovhlth/2011/highlights.html

9. This figure could be increased to 138 percent based upon use of Modified Adjusted Gross Income as established by the PPACA.

Chapter 2

1. National Federation of Independent Business v. Sebelius, 567 US _____ (2012)

2. 26 USC §7421(a)

3. Article 1, Section 8, Clause 3 of the United States Constitution

4. Article 1, Section 8, Clause 18 of the United States Constitution

5. NFIB v. Sebelius

6. Ibid.

7. Ibid.

8. Article 1, Section 8, Clause 1 of the United States Constitution

9. Article 1, Section 9, Clause 4 of the United States Constitution

10. Article 1, Section 8, Clause 1 of the United States Constitution

11. This figure could be increased to 138 percent based upon use of Modified Adjusted Gross Income as established by the PPACA.

12. NFIB v. Sebelius

13. Ibid.

14. Katheryn Jean Lopez, "Cardinal Dolan on Assault on Religious Freedom: Not a Slippery Slope, But a Ski Slope," National Review Online. http ://www.nationalreview.com/corner/349481/cardinal-dolan-threats -continuing-conscience-were-talking-about-ski-slopes-not

Chapter 4

1. Neil Tseng, "Expenditures on Entertainment," Consumer Expenditure Survey Anthology, 2003.
http://www.bls.gov/cex/anthology/csxanth10.pdf

2. Damon Darlin, "How to Tame an Inflated Budget," New York Times.
http://www.nytimes.com/2005/11/19/business/19money.html?pagewanted=all&_r=0

3. Hubert Janicki, "Employment-Based Health Insurance: 2010," US Census Bureau. http://www.census.gov/prod/2013pubs/p70-134.pdf

4. This figure could be increased to 138 percent based upon use of Modified Adjusted Gross Income as established by the PPACA.

5. Darlin, "How to Tame an Inflated Budget."

Chapter 5

1. Richard E. Schumann, "Compensation from World War II through the Great Society," Bureau of Labor and Statistics. http://www.bls.gov/opub/cwc/cm20030124ar04p1.htm

2. "About the Blue Cross and Blue Shield Association," Blue Cross Blue Shield. http://www.bcbs.com/about-the-association/

3. Dorothy P. Rice and Barbara S. Cooper, "National Health Expenditures, 1929-71." http://socialsecurity.gov/policy/docs/ssb/v35n1/v35n1p3.pdf

Chapter 8

1. "Highlights 2011," US Census Bureau.
   http://socialsecurity.gov/policy/docs/ssb/v35n1/v35n1p3.pdf

Chapter 9

1. PPACA Section 1501

2. National Federation of Independent Business v. Sebelius, 567 US
   _____ (2012)

3. "State-level unions demand ObamaCare fix, as Obama meets labor
   leaders," Fox News.
   http://www.foxnews.com/politics/2013/09/13/state-level-unions -line-
   up-behind-afl-cio-to-oppose-parts-obamacare/

4. Jason Miller, "Miller: Employers will figure out ways to dodge
   Obamacare," http ://www.foxnews.com/politics/2013/09/13/state-
   level-unions -line-up-behind-afl-cio-to-oppose-parts-obamacare/

Chapter 10

1. PPACA Section 1501

2. National Federation of Independent Business v. Sebelius, 567 US _____ (2012)

3. PPACA Section 1302

4. Additional complicating factors will occur as well. For instance, the increased cost of providing "qualified" coverage will come into play. Premium rate shock will also lead to increases in cost.

5. "Opinion Research Poll," CNN. http://i2.cdn.turner.com/cnn/2010/images/03/22/rel5b.pdf

6. This amount is weak compared to the cost of coverage but is still meaningful to individuals and families now forced to pay this new tax. Also, consistent with the overall theme of the PPACA, the penalty increases each year so the full sting will not be felt up front.

7. "2013 Poverty Guidelines," US Department of Health and Human Services. http://aspe.hhs.gov/poverty/13poverty.cfm

8. This figure is based upon 2013 averages, which is before the majority of Obamacare's requirements will have been implemented. Premium rate shock will mean much higher prices for 2014, and as employers drop coverage and individuals game the system, with fewer individuals in the private market and with the risk pool devoid of many of the "good risk" individuals, the long-term impact on rates will widen the divide between the price of compliance with the PPACA and the price of the penalty.

9. "2013 Employer Health Benefits Survey," Kaiser Family Foundation. http://kff.org/private-insurance/report/2013-employer-health-benefits/

10. Richard S. Foster, Chief Actuary, Centers for Medicare & Medicaid Services, "Estimated Financial Effects of the 'Patient Protection and Affordable Care Act,' as Amended," Centers for Medicare & Medicaid Services. https://www.cms.gov/ActuarialStudies/Downloads/PPACA_2010-04-22.pdf

11. Ibid.

12. Ibid.

13. PPACA Section 1501

14. "Hatch Statement on Obama Administration's Decision to Delay Health Law's Job-Killing Employer Mandate." http://www.hatch.senate.gov/public/index.cfm/releases?ID=9d9a004 b-52f8-491c-ab4c-b377d3ab8cb3

Chapter 11

1. "Highlights 2009," US Census Bureau.
    http://www.census.gov/hhes/www/hlthins/data/incpovhlth/2009/highl
    ights.html

2. This figure could be increased to 138 percent based upon use of
    Modified Adjusted Gross Income as established by the PPACA.

Chapter 13

1. "Highlights 2009," US Census Bureau.
    http://www.census.gov/hhes/www/hlthins/data/incpovhlth/2009/highl
    ights.html

2. "Highlights 2009, 2010, 2011," US Census Bureau.
    http://www.census.gov/hhes/www/hlthins/data/incpovhlth/2009/highl
    ights.html;
    http://www.census.gov/hhes/www/hlthins/data/incpovhlth/2010/highl
    ights.html;
    http://www.census.gov/hhes/www/hlthins/data/incpovhlth/2011/highl
    ights.html

3. This figure could be increased to 138 percent based upon use of
    Modified Adjusted Gross Income as established by the PPACA.

4. This figure could be increased to 138 percent based upon use of
    Modified Adjusted Gross Income as established by the PPACA.

5. Figure 13.2 is based upon the amounts established for the contiguous
    forty-eight states. The Office of the Assistant Secretary for Planning
    and Evaluation published specific amounts applicable to Alaska and
    Hawaii.

6. "2013 Poverty Guidelines," US Department of Health and Human
    Services, Office of the Assistant Secretary for Planning and Evaluation.
    http://aspe.hhs.gov/poverty/13poverty.cfm

7. This figure could be increased to 138 percent based upon use of
    Modified Adjusted Gross Income as established by the PPACA.

8. Rep. Fred Upton, "The Looming Premium Rate Shock," US House of
    Representatives Committee on Energy and Commerce. http
    ://energycommerce.house.gov/sites/republicans.energycommerce
    .house.gov/files/analysis/insurancepremiums/FinalReport.pdf

9. Ibid.

10. "2013 Poverty Guidelines," US Department of Health and Human Services. http://aspe.hhs.gov/poverty/13poverty.cfm

Chapter 15

1. "NIH Budget," National Institutes of Health.
   http://www.nih.gov/about/budget.htm

2. "Estimates of Funding for Various Research, Condition, and Disease
   Categories (RCDC)," National Institutes of Health.
   http://report.nih.gov/categorical_spending.aspx

3. Leigh Page, "New Three-Year Track Seeks to Boost Family Medicine,
   Reduce Student Debt," American Association of Medical Colleges.
   https://www.aamc.org/newsroom/reporter/october2012/308506/fami
   ly-medicine.html

4. Laura Fletcher, "Competition for Entrance to Medical Schools."
   http://everydaylife.globalpost.com/competition-entrance-medical-
   schools-19258.html

CPSIA information can be obtained at www.ICGtesting.com
Printed in the USA
BVOW01s0338241213

340010BV00001B/65/P